THANK GOD I PAID CASH FOR THE ROLLS!

STORIES OF FINANCIAL STRUGGLE, SURVIVAL AND SUCCESS

WELLINGTON PRESS

ERIC S BALL

ISBN: 0-9846895-0-8

ISBN-13: 978-0-9846895-0-7

DISCLAIMERS:

The opinions expressed in this book are those of the author only and are intended as general information only and not specific investment advice. Readers are advised to consult with licensed professionals in their state for specific legal, tax, accounting and investment advice.

Discussion of investment products which are sold by a prospectus, have been intentionally omitted to comply with regulatory requirements.

All names and places referenced in this book are fictitious, except where noted. All stories (except for the legend of "The Three Travelers") are based upon actual events and the author's personal experiences and observations. Names, places and some details and descriptions have been changed or modified to provide confidentiality.

Eric S. Ball is a Registered Representative with and Securities and Advisory services are offered through KMS Financial Services, Inc.

Member FINRA/SIPC

For
Mom and Dad

ACKNOWLEDGEMENTS:

The author is very grateful for the contribution and support
of many gifted people in the creation of this book:

Trudy Triner, Beth Proudfoot, Howard Miller, Johanna Small,
Carlos Rivas, Ted Moore, Rob Taylor, Donna Juvet, Ruth Ball,
John Supino, Buck Shaffer, Eric Jansen, Craig Vejvoda, Jim
Barton, Lon Tanner, Jean Schore, John Manning, Paul Hoagland

TABLE OF CONTENTS

PROLOGUE

IN FROM THE LEDGE – A FINANCIAL PLANNER'S NIGHTMARE

September 15th, 2008. The flashing red lights on the computer screen signaled the stock market was tanking. Doom and gloom and disaster were everywhere. Decades worth of hard work by clients to save and accumulate was wiped out in weeks...days...minutes.

The phone rang. A glance at the caller ID showed it was from my broker-dealer's margin department. There could be only one reason for the telephone call; it was a margin call for the account of Al and Sue Johnson who had borrowed against their stocks. Now those stocks had dropped in value; Al and Sue were forced to come up with money to save the stocks, or they would have to be sold at a loss.

To make matters worse, the check had to be sent, a photocopy of the check faxed, and a tracking number from the overnight delivery service provided within the hour or else! Drop everything and get it done now!

I called the client and said, "Al, we've got to come up with $10,000 more for your account." It had to be put in right then, right there, right away! We had already met three margin calls during the previous week, totaling nearly $20,000. Fortunately, Al and Sue had another source of funds they could easily access, and the margin call could be met. Sue would bring the check to the office in 20 minutes.

Meanwhile, my own account had troubles. I, too, had borrowed against my stocks when I bought my house during the hyper - inflated real estate run-up for a bit more than I should have spent for the old pile of lumber on the wrong side of the tracks in Cold City, California. I also had to send a check that day – for $2,000 from another line of credit – the third check I had sent in that week.

I took my check with the client's check, and walked out to the parking lot to take the overnight envelope to UPS.

And there it sat, the car I had dreamed about for 30 years, the car I had saved my money for and bought as a "previously owned" car when it was 18 years old, the car I had read about, gone to shows and club events, and gleaned tons of advice about which model to buy, which model to avoid, and how much to figure for maintenance.

I slipped behind the wheel of my 1989 Rolls-Royce Silver Spur, turned the key in the walnut burl dashboard, and looked through the windscreen over the bonnet to the Spirit of Ecstasy, her wings spread into the wind, proudly soaring atop the classic grill. It struck me as ironic, almost macabre, that there I was, ready to drive down the road to financial Armageddon in a Rolls-Royce!

As a financial planner, it was up to me to know what to say, how to provide certainty and how to calm my clients in an uncertain world. In that moment, though, with the stock market cratering and my stomach churning, all I could think to say to myself was, "Thank God I paid cash for the Rolls!"

After a quick trip to the local UPS store, the deed was done. The margin call was met again, the stocks were saved for another day, and now it was back to the office, and back to the computer screen with its blinking red light and a crashing stock market.

On the drive back to the office, I thought about all the clients with 401(k) plans, or stock and bond portfolios who would be calling in the next few days, weeks and months ahead, asking "What will I do now? How will I manage through this melt down!?"

You see, the Rolls was the culmination of a long-held childhood dream. For more than 30 years, I had dreamed about owning one of these magnificent cars. I was a member of the Rolls-Royce Owner's Club for 10 years before I ever bought my 'pre-owned' 1989 Silver Spur. But I had done it right. I had waited and saved for the car, and I had bought an older one in good condition that I could both afford to purchase and to maintain.

During times of economic turmoil, it is important to look at how we got where we are and to come up with a game plan for going forward. We must calmly review not just what we have done wrong, but also what we have done right. We must remind ourselves that economic cycles are inevitable, and while others may be "freaking out", we lay plans to make the best of, perhaps even take advantage of, the current downturn.

I have written this book to give you practical, usable ideas, tips and tools to help minimize the pain of economic upheavals and take advantage of opportunities so that you can not only survive, but thrive, in good times and bad.

Let me also make a comment about the Rolls; some readers may be put off by something that is, strictly speaking, not a necessity. I could launch into a plausible argument that having an automobile that is built to last for decades (with upkeep) and is always a thing of great beauty is a better use of resources than the planned obsolescence model wherein one must buy a new car every three or five years because either the thing is worn out or worse yet, one must "keep up with the Joneses". In reality, it is a bit of an extravagance, based upon an emotional response. Let the idea and concept of a Rolls-Royce serve as a place holder for a specific goal or achievement, whether it is material or self development, which is something that is meaningful to you, lasting, satisfying and always a joy. It need not be terribly expensive, but it may very well be something that took effort and determination to achieve. So identify your equivalent of a "Rolls-Royce" and use the ideas in this book to help you work toward that end.

This book will help you review what has worked and what hasn't in your financial life, and offers a number of concrete strategies to attain and enjoy financial freedom.

ACTION STEPS:

- Determine your personal "Rolls-Royce".

- Let the idea and concept of the "Rolls" serve as shorthand for an achievement or goal that you want to accomplish. It may be a material item or a personal, educational, family or spiritual goal.

- Get clear on that ideal and use the ideas and inspiration from the people in this book to work toward your "Rolls".

* * *

A Brief History of Money

The signs were unmistakable. Demand was exceeding the supply. From November to February the contract price of the commodity kept going higher and higher until, at one point, the contracts sold for more than 10 times the annual income of the average worker. Everyone, it seems, wanted a piece of the action. Then, in February, traders suddenly found they could not find new buyers at the ever-rising prices. Demand vanished almost overnight, prices dropped; the contracts were now only a fraction of their old value. There was demand for government intervention.

Sound familiar? No, the year was not 2008 or even 1929. The year was 1637, the place was Holland, and the contracts were tulip bulb futures. In the nearly 400 years since the event that became known as "Tulip Mania", capitalist economies the world over have experienced boom and bust. We today are not the first and probably not the last to ride this roller coaster.

In the beginning there was money. And it was good. Money furnished human beings with currency, a method of exchange, rather than bartering. Money gave people both a store of value and a way to facilitate trading and exchanging goods, services, and labor. Over the centuries, elaborate banking systems, stock exchanges, insurance and investment structures all grew up surrounding money.

But let's put these relatively new and complicated systems aside for a moment and focus on a few basic principles about money that have applied throughout the ages.

The key to money is to always have enough so that if you are facing a difficult time, you do not have to make a huge sacrifice, and in good times you have enough money to take advantage of opportunities.

BOTTOM LINE

We are not the first (and sadly, probably not the last),
to experience boom and bust economic cycles.

ACTION STEPS:

- Prepare for the inevitable ebb and flow of the markets.

- Have a reserve that is not subject to market fluctuation.

- Have a contingency plan when you make a major purchase such as a home. Ask yourself, "What happens if I (and/or my spouse) loses a job, gets sick, or my business has a downturn?"

- Be careful not to "bet the ranch" on one financial transaction.

- Use only money you can live without for a period of time for riskier investments. That way, you won't have to cash out in a down market.

CHAPTER 1

PLANNING

Personal Capital

In the 21st century, it is more important than ever for each individual to be strong and financially independent. Historically, many people derived their financial security from their employer, their personal business, their union or the government. Although corporate America and state and federal governments will continue to play a role in our financial lives, none of us can afford to passively hold the belief that these institutions will always provide for us.

Each of us must think of our financial lives almost in a way that a charitable foundation approaches its mission. A typical charity will seek to build a pool of capital from which it can draw interest and earnings to pay its expenses and achieve its objectives. Just as a charity seeks to build an endowment fund, so too we, as individuals and families, must build our own **personal capital endowment** accounts.

Over a lifetime, each of us must build enough capital from a combination of personally owned and controlled capital along with Social Security and pension benefits provided by an employer.

Thank God I Paid Cash For The Rolls!

None of us can depend solely on Social Security or an employer's program alone to provide financial independence.

The goal for a personal capital endowment account is to build it to the point where the interest and earnings of your capital can provide for at least your basic standard of living and, in a perfect world, it can provide the "goodies" of life for you as well.

BOTTOM LINE

Although government and employer plans are a part of your overall plan, you are ultimately responsible for your financial well-being.

ACTION STEPS

- Develop your plan.

- Implement your plan

- Monitor your plan

Family Matters

Our family financial circumstances shape how we interact with money. The life and career of Benjamin N. "Woody" Woodson gives some great examples of this. Mr. Woodson was born in Kansas in 1909. He joined the life insurance industry in 1929, right at the start of the Great Depression. He started his career with the Life Insurance Marketing and Research Association (LIMRA). Then, he worked in what he described as the "Ivory Tower" of the home office of American General Life and rose to become its president and CEO.

Woody retired in 1979, but he continued as a broker working with businesses and individual clients during his 70s and well into his 80s. He lived to the ripe old age of 93.

During his so-called retirement years, he wrote a monthly column for an industry trade publication, Life Association News, entitled "The Back Page." It offered sage advice from someone who had lived through the Great Depression, World War II, and the expansion years of the 1950s and 60s.

Although I only met Mr. Woodson once, he had a great impact for many years on my professional development and understanding about money and more importantly, how money and planning impact one's family. When the magazine arrived at my office each month, I would literally turn to the back page and read Mr. Woodson's column first because his column and the advice therein was the single most valuable part of the entire publication.

At an annual convention of the National Association of Life Underwriters in Orlando, Florida in September, 1987, I was fortunate enough to meet my hero. As fate would have it, I attended the same breakfast meeting as Mr. Woodson, and suddenly, there I was standing face-to-face with this living legend. Desperately trying to say something halfway intelligent to this industry giant, I mentioned that I always read his column, "The Back Page", first. Mr. Woodson replied, "You keep reading. My attorney sues anyone who stops reading my column!" And indeed I did keep reading until he finally stopped writing the column in 1998.

Here are a couple of examples from Mr. Woodson's own life and experience that show how he served his family and the families of his clients:

In December of 1988, he reflected back on his oldest life insurance policy that he had purchased 59 years previously, in 1929:

"That policy was issued on December 4, 1929 which was the last day in all eternity that this applicant could qualify as a 21-year-old.

> *Therefore let it be noted and underlined the age change was then as it is today, one of those changes in circumstances which led to purchase and one of the most potent. But no further that this policy was issued in contemplation of an even greater, namely the awesome change from single blessedness to the still greater blessedness of marriage the sweet young lady had agreed (with some misgivings I have no doubt) to accept our wedding date for the following month and so quite naturally that proud new policy purchased in contemplation of marriage as well as age change became one of several Christmas gifts to the lady who became my wife in January of 1930." (Life Association News, December, 1988)*

* * *

This story is remarkable in that it demonstrates the particular maturity of a 21-year-old, head-over-heels in love with his young bride, yet wisely providing for her with what was a $5,000 face value life insurance policy, enough money to afford a house in 1929. Even in the giddiness of romance, Woody's life insurance purchase showed maturity and concern for the financial security of his wife.

It further demonstrated financial astuteness in that Woody bought the policy a day before an age change. That meant that the policy cost about 3% less in annual premiums than if he had waited one day more. Since that policy did not become a claim until Woody's death in 2001, some 72 years later, that was a very smart move indeed!

We now fast forward 12 years in Mr. Woodson's life. His wife had just given birth to a baby girl, the couple's first and only child. Let us focus on his actions on December 8, 1941. History records the momentous events of December 7th, 1941, Pearl Harbor Day. The very next day, Mr. Woodson had the foresight to put **two and two** together and take immediate action. He went out and bought **two** new insurance policies from **two** different carriers.

(That made sense at the time as he was working for the Life Insurance Marketing and Research Association (LIMRA). He couldn't play favorites so he bought two policies, from two different companies, rather than just one.)

Here is Mr. Woodson's own recollection of that day:

> *"My motivation for the purchase of these two policies was elementary. The nation was suddenly at war and I was of military age. In those circumstances I readily recognized the need for more life insurance. Moreover, I acted quickly in the hope of beating the prospective deadline of January 1, 1942, after which substantially all policies would bear the limitations and restrictions of the War Clause."*

(The War Clause meant that a policy would not pay, other than return of premium, if the insured died by an act of war. And sure enough, in the early years of my career I was assigned a Bankers Life policy to service for a man who became a very good client. His policy had been issued in 1943 and there, very boldly stamped on the face page of the policy, was indeed the very war clause that Mr. Woodson successfully avoided with his quick action in December of 1941.)

Mr. Woodson recognized that he might indeed be called to serve in the military, and that very soon new policies would be issued with the war clause, restricting the death benefit to his wife and young daughter; he took immediate and timely action.

Beyond just the dollars that his life insurance and financial planning represented, he did one more thing to ensure success and security for his family. Here again are his own words:

> *"The time soon came when Uncle Sam called me for examination for military service. I still have folded in with some of my policies a memorandum to the lady who was then my sweet wife. (Mrs. Woodson had passed on by the time these words were written in 1989) It was composed on the prior week. It was written to tell her what she should do to keep my policies in force and advise her as to what she and our baby daughter should do if my plane was shot down or my submarine failed to return or I stepped in front of an enemy bullet. And my ability to write that love letter and to know that all its instructions were as fully realistic gave me happiness and emotional stability beyond compare."*

"*Happiness and emotional stability beyond compare.*" That last phrase, that sentiment, should be the goal of everything we do surrounding money. With this goal in mind, we help ensure happiness and emotional stability for our own lives and for the lives of those we love.

Woody's story also demonstrates the importance of having two crucial ingredients of a good financial plan in place. In this case, in both Mr. Woodson's letter to his wife containing specific instructions along with the life insurance policies he had purchased to provide the money she would need in case of his death.

Let's take just a minute to examine what might have happened had Mr. Woodson died in action without both of those items in place. If he had died with no letter of instruction, no written plan for the life insurance policies, then those policies would have paid the claim to his wife and daughter who then would have had the money and who hopefully could have received wise advice from either a relative or trusted advisor who could have helped the widow and her child properly invest the money to take care of themselves. So if the funding, the money, were in place, Mrs. Woodson and her daughter would have had the financial resources to survive. Having the instruction letter, giving specific ideas about whom to call, what to do with the money, and how to structure things, would have made managing the money far easier.

However, let us examine what would have occurred if all that Mr. Woodson had left behind was a letter, without any life insurance policies or other source of funds or investments to back up his advice. The letter might have instructed his widow to consult a particular accountant, or ask financially astute Uncle Charlie how to manage things. All the best advice in the world would not have been as useful to a widow with a baby during World War II as having the cold hard cash.

Mr. Woodson's example of both creating the funding and providing the plan is the roadmap for all of us to emulate.

Even in today's world, where the plan may be very elaborate and the financing mechanisms not only life insurance policies, but a diversified investment portfolio, the bottom line is still the same: you must have both the plan and the money.

BOTTOM LINE

The goal of financial planning is to provide "happiness and emotional stability"

ACTION STEPS

- Develop a written plan.

- Have a qualified attorney prepare your will (and trust if appropriate). Make the hard decisions about who will manage your assets and look after minor children so your heirs won't have to make those sorts of choices.

- Start and build your investment portfolio, retirement plans and insurance programs.

Financial Timeline

Clients often ask what a person at a given age should be doing financially. The following chart, suggested by Jean Schore of Schore Marketing, is a guideline to the sorts of financial activity a person should be doing at a particular age. Of course, as in most things financial, there will be variations based on one's individual circumstances, but this timeline is a good general guideline.

Age 0-18 [Onus on parents here!] Learn about money and work; save for college

- Begin saving for college.

- Have children earn money, at an age-appropriate time, to begin understanding the relationship between effort and earning money.

- Drive home the point and need for your children to study and get a good education precisely so they won't have to do hard, physical, low-paid work as adults. (It is especially important for children of affluent parents to perform some work so that they understand that money does not come just from Dad's wallet or Mom's purse, or heaven forbid, the child's own credit card. Yikes!)

- Children should also be taught that money comes not only from clocked time (hourly wage), but also from intellect and/or ideas put into practice. This should be taught periodically.

- Children should be taught proper thrift and learn how to save. This is especially true if your child wants a very expensive "goody." Having the child work to earn at least part of the cost will make the item much more treasured. And, if the child won't work for it, perhaps it wasn't that important in the first place.

Teaching children about money

Children receive many messages about money while they are growing up. Some of it is very negative with comments like "Money doesn't grow on trees". Children get enormous pressure to become consumers very early with the latest toy, video game or fashionable clothes like the ones their friends have or what they see on television. The concept of "deferred gratification" which is hard enough for many adults to grasp is doubly hard for children who want things NOW!

That said, it is incumbent upon parents to teach and model the concepts of saving and working for a major goal. As a child, I had a paper route when I was 10 years old. It was tough work, especially collecting the subscription from some deadbeats, and I didn't net much money. However, when I "retired" from that profession, I did have enough to buy a very cool eight- band radio that had not only AM/FM, but two short wave bands, UHF, etc. I used that radio for years and it was a lasting tangible reward for delivering papers.

(As a side note, I used to dream about getting one of those console color TVs with the built-in stereo that were popular in the late 1960's. I used to figure out how many new subscriptions I would have to get to earn enough money to buy such a console. It was a good exercise in setting a goal and then figuring out how many sales it would take to earn the money. In reality, the amount of sales required far exceeded the number of people who might have bought the paper, but it was good to begin to develop the concept and not bad for a 10 year old to figure that out.)

A dilemma that many affluent parents struggle with is how much to do for their children. A parent may desire to see their children enjoying the nice things that maybe they didn't have at the same age, yet a well-meaning parent can cripple a child by handing everything to the child without the child learning at a gut level the effort required to earn the money, save it and then buy the item. In some cases, parents may feel guilty about not having enough time to spend with their children due to work or divorce and assuage that guilt with goodies.

It is not always necessary for the child to earn all of the money, but depending on what the item is, the parent may say to the child "If you earn $50.00, I will match the other $50.00 for this $100 item". This strategy might be particularly effective with older children or teenagers for a big-ticket item such as a car or a major school trip.

The key for parents is to teach their children the idea of setting a goal. The child learns what it takes to earn enough and how long. The key is to set these goals at a level that is age-appropriate for the child and an item for which the child has the capability of earning the money.

Age 19-25 — College

- Save, even if it is a tiny amount.

- Learn the basics of budgeting.

The college years are generally a period of net spending, since you are paying tuition and living expenses, very definitely a "wallet-emptying" exercise, whether parents are paying or the student is racking up hefty college loans. Additionally, students often work at low-wage part time jobs. The focus during this period is to study hard and earn the degree. It is a period of enforced frugality. However, learning how to manage on a tight budget can lay good groundwork and appreciation for managing money later in life, and hopefully for affluent years.

Age 26-35

- Ramp up the savings for a first home, children's college, e.g., other goals important to you.

- Pay off debts, including college loans, IF interest rates are higher than savings rates.

- Establish good budgeting habits.

- Insure your income with life and disability insurance.

The starting-out years are a good time to set financial patterns that will serve you well over time. With luck and perseverance, you are finally out of college and working full-time. There may be some temptation to overspend, now that you have a regular paycheck. Follow the 5% Fun Rule, meaning don't spend more than 5% of your income on things that are "nice to have" but not strictly necessary That will give you some goodies, but keep you from getting over-extended with credit cards. Focus on saving money since these dollars will have the chance to earn a return for you for 30 or 40 years or more. As you furnish an apartment or home, ramp up over time, buying the most important items as you can afford them and "making do" with a few hand-me-downs and thrift store treasures. Later, as finances permit, you can upgrade to swankier "stuff."

Age 36-50

- Build your career.

- Start your own business and/or continue professional development.

- Diversify your savings.

- Plan for children's college if you didn't start earlier.

*These are the **run hard** years. Put your shoulder to the wheel, but keep life in balance. And don't forget to enjoy life as you go along.*

Age 51-60

- Pay for children's college.

- Run career/business.

- Have your assets still primarily set for growth, but begin to position some for stability of principal.

- Evaluate second or third career.

- Increase savings levels.

*This is the period when many people are at their **peak earning years**. Now is the time to get financially strong for retirement, regardless of when you plan to stop or slow down work. The more you save, the more options you will have.*

Age 61-65 Plan for "Golden Years"

- Get clear on when/how to retire/ continue to work, or begin a second career.

- Position assets for income first and some for growth.

- Consider long-term care insurance.

- Get clear on what you want to do with your "Golden Years"; this is when you begin planning for those years. The more you have planned and saved (and yes, ate healthy food, exercised, didn't smoke, and wore your seat belt), the more golden those years will be for you.

Age 66-80

- Work or play as desired.

- Plan for legacy/charity bequests.

- Position assets towards income production. Keep some assets positioned for growth.

    The key for the early part of retirement is to keep active, whether income-producing work, volunteer work, hobby or pastime that you really enjoy. Socialize with people of all ages, as that keeps you involved with the world around you and makes life more interesting. So enjoy your Golden Years!

Age 80-120 (Yes, 120! That's what the latest mortality charts say!)

- Pass on your wisdom, "life lessons learned" to your heirs.

- Keep as active as possible.

- Live at home as long as possible.

My great uncle, Olin Jacoby, lived to be 101 years old and was in very good health right up to the last month of his life. He had founded Golden West Savings and Loan in the 1929 and had made a go of it, even in tough times. As a retired financial type in his 90s and 100s, each morning he would add up a column of numbers with a paper and pen and then check the total with a calculator. This was his way of making sure his mind was still sharp... and it was!

Aging is an entire subject unto itself, but given that people who have taken care of themselves will very likely live into the 80's, 90's or even past 100, it becomes all the more important to have both sufficient capital and a written plan. We cannot control the genetic factors in our life, or the passage of time, but by having enough money and planning, you can have more and better options for care and quality of life than someone who is at the mercy of a government program (or a slacker relative!).

Single seniors need a chain of reliable, younger people to look after them. They may be relatives, friends, professionals or a combination thereof. Be sure to have backups, as even younger people get older, too!

Steps to take

Here are the basic steps to sound financial planning:

- Set your financial goals – short, mid, long-range and lifetime.
- Take stock of what you already have.

- Start systematically saving or, if already saving, increase the amount of your savings.

- Monitor investments and make changes as appropriate.

- Understand and use debt and credit wisely and carefully.

- Set a plan to eliminate, or at least reduce, debt.

- Plan for purchases, look for good value.

- "The Implementation Gap" - Managing Procrastination. (See Chapter 3)

- Create a Personal Capital Endowment.

What does "Retirement" look like for you?

Standard retirement age used to be 65 because that was the age at which Social Security would begin paying benefits. But our ideas about retirement and retirement age – especially with the solvency of Social Security threatened – have changed. Therefore, the more that you can create your own financial autonomy, the more choices you will have as to when and how you retire.

Today, some people, regardless of their income and assets, may still enjoy working for the psychological benefit it provides, for the challenge of their careers and for a sense of purpose and usefulness well past age 65. Others may have a more compelling desire to pursue a different career or a hobby, do charitable work or spend more time with their families. A third group may no longer be physically able to work and simply must retire. Finally, a fourth group may have to continue working past age 65 because they need the income just to survive. The whole purpose of this book, however, is to help you avoid joining this fourth group.

The examples below will give you two sides of the spectrum, showing that there is no longer a set age of retirement:

I had one client, Harold Fairway, a citrus grower, who retired at age 60 and moved to a beautiful home on the third fairway of a country club. He and his wife played golf at least six times a week for the next nearly 30 years. This was the life that appealed to him and he was successful from that standpoint. (Harold, by the way, walked the entire course each day rather than riding in a golf cart.)

Another client Myron Maison, retired from teaching school in his 60s, and since then, for the past 20 years, has worked as a real estate agent. He has frequently been the top producer in his office. Even when he first retired from teaching, he had sufficient assets and pension income so he could have retired and never worked again a day in his life. In fact, he continues to be a net saver rather than a net spender. For Myron, the stimulation of working provides meaning for his life and he would be absolutely bored to tears if he were to sit in the proverbial rocking chair – or play golf six times a week.

BOTTOM LINE

Get crystal clear about what retirement should look like for you. Work like crazy to make it a reality.

The lesson from both of these clients is that they each had the assets to live on without having to work for an income. One chose to pursue a lifelong hobby and the other preferred work, for the sake of the challenge, not the need for the income.

ACTION STEPS

- Determine what you want to do in retirement.

- Couples should communicate with each other about their individual aspirations for retirement.

The Long-term Perspective

It is human nature to make short term choices that can be detrimental for the long-term. With money, it is critical to focus on making decisions that are best in the long-term even if that choice is more difficult or requires a sacrifice in the short term.

In many cases, especially with stock values, it will often be a combination of actual problems, their consequences, and an overreaction by investors.

An issue that is now seemingly a permanent part of our society is the 24-hour news cycle, combined with the internet. The result is a cornucopia of information, which is not necessarily pertinent, germane or useful. There is a huge tendency for media to report more "heat" than "light"; and much of our news comes with a built-in editorial viewpoint on all sides of the political spectrum.

The result is that bad news can be overstated so that we all end up in despair and good news can be "hyped" which may lead to a euphoria that is not grounded in reality.

"Short Term Pain for Long Term Gain"

Suppose that on April 14 your accountant informs you that you owe more income tax than you thought you would have to pay. Your CPA suggests that by contributing $5,000 into an IRA account, you would save $1,500 in state and federal income tax if your tax bracket is a combined 30%. So you make the sacrifice of taking $5,000 out of savings or checking, as I have done on more than one occasion. Making the $5,000 contribution gives you a $1500 tax savings, so the net cost is only $3500, yet you have $5,000 in the IRA account that will now grow tax-deferred until you begin to withdraw it years or decades later.

In the short run, you might prefer to have the $5,000 to spend or enjoy, but you'll thank yourself that you saved the money and that you've saved the income tax.

If you are 40 years old and keep that $5,000 contribution in the account until age 70, at 5% annual interest, your $5,000 will become approximately $20,000, and you'll thank yourself for having made the sacrifice some 30 years earlier.

The importance of a long-term perspective becomes even more crucial during periods of uncertainty, volatility and panic. In these times, you as the investor must step back and analyze how much of the current crisis is valid and how much is the result of a perceived short-term calamity fueled by hysteria.

BOTTOM LINE

Do the right things, take the necessary timely action, and take the "short term pain" for the long-term gain.

ACTION STEPS

- Focus.

- Get consistent at becoming pro-active.

Main Street, 30 Years Later

I point the hood of the car south on Main St. and drive past the stores. It's my hometown but it could be your hometown, anyone's hometown in any small town or medium-sized city in the US. I think about how little has changed and yet how much has changed over the past 30 years since I moved back here in the early 1980s. Physically most of the same buildings are here and most of them look the same. There's one or two new buildings and a couple of odd remodels but by and large the Main Street of the early 21st century looks like the close of the last century.

But as I drive by the buildings, I think about the people and the businesses that used to occupy those buildings. Thirty years later, very few are still owned by the same people. Some are gone because the owners reached a certain age and retired. Others, like the old hardware store, are gone because they couldn't compete with the new big-box stores at the edge of town.

Some of these businesses were very successful in their day and their owners carefully saved their money, built retirement accounts and investment portfolios and retired comfortably. Some have since passed that wealth on to their children and grandchildren. Others always found it a struggle for one reason or another.

The key component for every last one was change. Very few of these business owners are doing today what they were doing 30 years ago. In the space of 30 years all these people embarked on a dream, ran their business successfully or unsuccessfully, and then retired or sold out or sadly, in a few cases, passed on. But in every single case there was always a need for planning and a need to recognize that today's reality would change to tomorrow's new reality and circumstances.

Thank God I Paid Cash For The Rolls!

The stationery store. Bill Blotter owned the store and his outside salesman, John Fellingham, would come around once a week to see what stationary and supplies we needed. We would place our order, and the next day the delivery man would show up with paper, pencils, file folders, etc. Later John died and then Bill retired. Bill's two daughters carried on for a while but when they lost a big school contract to a big-box store their business was over.

The hardware store. The Belton family had run an old-time hardware store in the same location for close to 80 years. A brother and sister had run it, and later a nephew and a son and cousins ran the business. As is often the case, one partner, Abe Belton was a good solid businessman and the other partner sadly looked upon the business only as a personal ATM machine to supply cash for whatever frivolous pickup truck or trip was on the must-have list that day.

The diner. Joe and Julie Bozeman ran Joe's Café. Joe handled the duties in the kitchen while Julie seated the customers managed the waitresses and carefully counted and saved the money. Every lunch hour they had a special of the day and on Thursdays the line was out the door with people ordering the special tostada. Thanksgiving and Christmas time saw the little restaurant with stacks of pink high boxes waiting to be filled with homemade pumpkin and pecan pies. Finally one day they sold the diner and moved up near the country club and the golf course.

Is the small town retail merchant going to disappear from the American scene? Only time will tell the answer. But what those 30 years prove is the need to save, to plan, and to recognize that circumstances will change.

CHAPTER 2

THE POWER OF SAVING

The Legend of the Three Travelers

"There is a legend of three travelers who journeyed under a hot, blazing sun across the desert. As nightfall approached, they saw palm trees in the distance, and soon came to an oasis. Through the middle of the oasis ran a little stream with pebbles on the bottom.

As the travelers began to set up camp for the night, a stranger on horseback appeared on the other side of the stream. The three travelers tensed and prepared to fight, fearing that the stranger might be a bandit. But the stranger held up his hand and said, "Fear not, I come in peace and with good tidings. Bend down and fill your pockets with pebbles from this stream."

Although the travelers were perplexed at this odd request, they did as the stranger commanded and filled their pockets with pebbles. When they had finished, the stranger said, "Tomorrow morning, you will be both glad and sad." And with that, he turned his horse and rode off into the night.

When the travelers awoke the next morning, they reached their hands into their pockets and were astonished to find that the pebbles had turned into rubies, diamonds, emeralds, and gems of every description. And they were indeed both glad and sad. Glad they had taken what they had, and sad that they had not taken more". (Life Association News, May, 1981)

That is the eternal story of money and saving. Most of us don't realize what amounts our savings can grow into. You will always be glad later about what you have saved today, and always be a bit sad that you did not save more; focus on saving as much as possible today and expanding your savings tomorrow.

Two Circles

Take a look at the two circles. In the circle on the left are the people who save first and then spend what is left over. In the circle on the right are those who spend first and then save what is left over, if any. The people in the right-hand circle always end up working for the people in the left-hand circle. In which circle do you want to be?

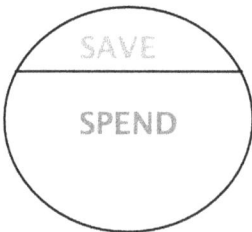

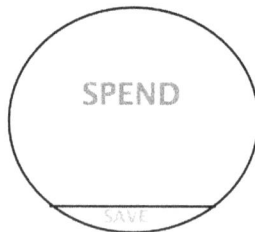

Two Circles

Which Circle Do You Want to Be

The most important concept about managing money is to always **spend less than you earn**. Or, as George Clauson put it his novel, *The Richest Man in Babylon*: "A part of all I earn is mine to keep."

This is the basic principle upon which all other discussions about money depend. Deciding when to save, when to spend, when to invest and what kinds of investments you make are all ultimately grounded in this simple, single principle of spending less than you earn.

Another sage once put it, "Happiness is spending a nickel less than you make and misery is spending a nickel more than you make."

BOTTOM LINE

Save a part of every paycheck.

WHICH CIRCLE DO YOU WANT TO BE IN?

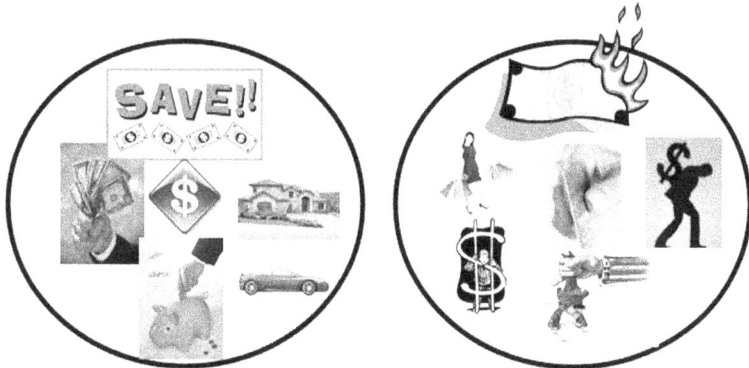

WEALTH   DEBT

I have experienced the power of this principle first-hand in my own life, and I have observed it in countless situations working with clients. The outcomes for those who adhered to this principle were vastly different than for those who did not. The people who saved had money for opportunities as they came along, and were seldom if ever in crisis situations where they were overextended and forced by debt to make undesirable decisions. The opposite is true for those who did not save adequately or had consistently lived far beyond their means. When a speed bump or pothole appeared in the financial road of life, as it will to most of us at some point, they were severely jolted, at best, if not run off the road entirely.

Now at this stage, let me emphasize that very few people always make every financial decision perfectly. Very few have always saved consistently or made the best financial decision in every circumstance. We are not looking for, nor should we expect, perfection, rather we are looking for consistency, doing the right thing, year in and year out, with plans and goals in mind that give us a lifeline when times are at their worst.

Make Saving Easy

The key to successfully saving is to make it easy and automatic. For most people, this means some sort of payroll deduction, typically through one's employer into a 401(k), 403 (b) or some other retirement program.

One can also save systematically with a credit union or bank, arranging to have a certain amount automatically transferred from your checking account into savings each month. You can also set up automatic payment plans for cash value life insurance policies, deferred annuities, brokerage accounts, and IRA accounts.

The key in all cases is to have the savings occur either at the point you get the funds, such as your paycheck, or second best, out of your checking account. This way you will always pay yourself first.

As you can imagine, it is much easier to be self-disciplined when you set yourself up for success. With an automatic savings plan, you only make the decision once, rather than every month or every paycheck when it's easy to put it off or convince yourself that "just this time" you really need to spend that cash now.

For self-employed people, this will require a bit more discipline, especially for those who do not get regular paychecks or take a regular draw. For the self-employed, having a business account fund an IRA automatically, for example, may increase the odds of successfully saving.

BOTTOM LINE

Even when it is tough, get started saving and planning.

ACTION STEPS:

- Set up an automatic savings plan through your bank, credit union or a payroll savings plan at work.

- Use your employer's retirement plan for automatic long-term savings, to get the benefit of any employer match, and to enjoy the benefit of tax deferred compound interest.

- Decide to not withdraw money from your savings account unless it's an absolute emergency.

- Spend less than you earn.

- Set goals and take action to complete those goals.

The Magic of Compound Interest –The Single Mom

Linda Chateau was excited to be working "on the platform" as a junior loan officer at Mountain Community Bank. As a single mother with three youngsters at home, her new job gave her a glimmer of hope. I had met Linda through the Chamber of Commerce and in my role as the 401(k) advisor to the bank's 401(k) plan.

BOTTOM LINE

Compound Interest is one of the most powerful financial tools. Make compound interest work for you.

"It's really hard for me to save right now", said Linda, 'I am single with three children; and it's tough to make ends meet." I encouraged Linda to start the plan at just 1% of salary. "Try it for a few paychecks", I said "That way you will get some of the bank's matching funds as well as your contribution. Then, increase the contribution as you are able."

The years turned into a decade. Over time, Linda was promoted several times, became a department head and later the branch manager of the largest branch in the firm. She even got married again. As her pay increased, she increased her contribution to the 401(k) plan. It was encouraging to see her progress at the annual plan review. Her plan has grown to well over $250,000 and still grows to this day.

She said to me, "I am so glad you encouraged me to get started all those years ago, even when it was so difficult. Now, I tell my story to all the people who work for me at the bank, to encourage them to get started.

"Baby Dollars Creating Baby Dollars" – The Magic of Compound Interest

Close behind the importance of systematic savings comes the second most important financial principle, the magic and power of compound interest. If you have $1000 in a bank account and it earns 5%, at the end of one year you have earned $50 and the account balance is now $1050. The next year, your account will earn $52.50 – $50 interest on the initial $1000 plus $2.50 interest on the $50 interest earned in the first year. This is a basic example of compound interest, or as we occasionally say in the "oh so sophisticated" world of high finance, "baby dollars creating baby dollars."

The key to taking advantage of compound interest is having the discipline and ability to let the earnings stay and gain more interest, whether they are reinvested in the same account or reallocated into another investment. When combined with tax deferral, as is generally the case with qualified retirement plans, or if tax-free, as in the case of municipal bonds, Roth IRA and Roth 401(k), the results are further magnified.

RULE OF 72

RATE OF RETURN	RULE OF 72	ACTUAL NUMBER OF YEARS TO DOUBLE
3%	24	23.45
4%	18	17.67
5%	14.4	14.21
6%	12	11.90
7%	10.29	10.24
8%	9	9.01
9%	8	8.04
10%	7.2	7.27
11%	6.54	6.64
12%	6	6.12
13%	5.54	5.67
14%	5.14	5.29
15%	4.8	4.96

BOTTOM LINE

Investments and assets that grow on a tax-deferred
basis get the benefit of earnings on money that
would otherwise have been paid in taxes.

ACTION STEPS:

- Leave any money in your savings account and investments alone. Let the magic of compound interest do its work.

The Rule of 72

A quick shorthand for calculating how fast money will double is called the "Rule of 72." You simply divide the annual interest rate by 72 to get the number of years it takes for money to double at that interest rate (assuming that you make that exact rate of return for the entire period and that you let the interest compound, rather than withdraw it along the way).

If an account earns 10%, your money will double in 7.2 years, 10 divided by 72. The chart shown gives a quick shortcut for rates of return from 3% to 15%.

Tax Deferral

Tax deferral allows the owner of an asset to defer paying income tax on gain (increase in value) or interest until a later date. This is a typical feature of 401(k) s and other pension plans.

Tax deferral and interest compounding together make a powerful financial combination. Tax deferral is especially effective when you have control over when you start receiving the accrued assets as taxable income. Look for ways to create accounts that provide tax deferral. Pension accounts are particularly attractive in this regard in that the investor can make changes from one investment to another without having to pay current income tax as long as the funds all remain under the qualified plan umbrella. This ability to change investments without having to consider the tax ramifications from selling one investment to buy another adds a tremendous amount of flexibility.

A second type of tax deferral is an asset that has unrealized capital gains. This might be shares of stock or a piece of real estate which has appreciated. The owner will pay tax when the asset is sold and the gain realized. You then control when to recognize the tax, since you decide when and how to sell the asset.

Under certain circumstances, however, you can exchange one piece of real estate for another qualifying property without having to pay current capital gains tax on the first property. Your basis in the new property will be carried over from the first so that if you subsequently sell the second property, you will pay your capital gain then. This is called a Section 1031 exchange and can be extremely helpful if you are selling a property, buying a similar property and you follow the proscribed legal rules for the transaction. Always consult with a qualified tax advisor before attempting a Section 1031 exchange to ensure that the proposed transaction qualifies under the rules.

Many sell or hold decisions are based upon the capital gain tax implications. Some people simply do not want to pay capital gain tax and would rather leave the property to their heirs, since the heirs will get "step up in basis" upon the owner's death.

"Step up in basis" works in this manner. Suppose Grandpa Greenthumb purchased a 100 acre farm in 1950 for $200 per acre. He paid $20,000. The $20,000 figure is known as the "cost basis"

By the year 2005, the farm was now valued at $1,000 per acre for a total of $100,000. If Grandpa sold the farm that year, he would have a long-term capital gain of $80,000 ($100,000 sale price minus $20,000 original purchase price) Grandpa would have had long-term capital gains tax due on the $80,000 gain. If the federal long-term capital gain tax rate is 15%, Grandpa would owe tax of $12,000 ($80,000 x 15% = $12,000). Grandpa would also owe any applicable state income tax. So if Grandpa sells during his lifetime, he pays some tax.

Let us suppose that Grandpa did not sell the farm, died in 2006 and left the farm to his grandson, Greenbean. The farm was appraised at $100,000 as of the date of Grandpa's death. The $100,000 value of the farm now becomes Grandson Greenbean's cost basis. The cost basis has "stepped up" from Grandpa's $20,000 to Grandson's $100,000. If Grandson sells the property for $100,000, he has no capital gains tax. If Grandson holds the property for at least one year and then sells it, he only pays long-term capital gains tax on the appreciation over the $100,000 mark. This strategy works if the owner does not need the assets for another purpose during his or her lifetime.

ACTION STEPS:

- Use qualified retirement plans as appropriate to your situation.

- Understand the tax implications of short and long-term capital gains and how they impact your investments.

Tax-Free

Few things in the financial world are truly tax-free, legally. However, there are three instruments that investors should consider, especially investors who are in a high marginal tax bracket and expect to remain so. The first is a tax-free municipal bond, the second is a Roth IRA and the third is a Roth 401(k).

Tax-free municipal bonds are issued by state and local governments and by entities such as a hospital or water district. By statute, the interest from these bonds is exempt from taxes, or tax-free, for federal income tax purposes, and generally will be state income tax-free for taxpayers who are residents of the state where the bond is issued.

BOTTOM LINE

Tax free is good!

Often investors will buy only those municipal bonds issued by the state in which they reside, so that they will not have to pay state income tax on the interest from those bonds. For example, a New York state resident will buy municipal bonds issued only by New York state or a municipality in that state. This is done to reduce the cost of the state income tax. The downside of this strategy is that the investor will hold all of the bonds in one state only. From a diversification standpoint, it may make more sense for the investor to buy some municipal bonds that are not issued in the taxpayer's home state. The trade-off in losing the state income tax savings is potentially mitigated by having a greater geographic diversification of the portfolio.

The Roth IRA and Roth 401(k) are recent developments that provide no current income tax deduction when the funds are contributed, but if taken properly, allow tax-free income when the funds are withdrawn. The general rule of thumb about either of the Roth IRA or the Roth 401(k) is that they are most effective for the person who anticipates that he or she will be in a high tax bracket when the funds are withdrawn. Where applicable, these accounts can make sense even for the wealthy taxpayer who would otherwise buy municipal bonds. The benefit of a Roth IRA or Roth 401(k) is that the investor gets the tax-free treatment with a greater choice of investments rather than only having the option of municipal bonds.

Roth IRAs

The Roth IRA was first authorized in the Pension Act of 1996. When properly structured the Roth IRA can provide a tax-free income, meaning there is no income tax on the earnings in the account. The only disadvantage of the Roth IRA is that income earners above a certain level of adjusted gross income may not make a contribution on an annual basis nor be able to affect a Roth IRA conversion.

For taxpayers who are below the Roth IRA limits (in tax year 2012 the limits were $125,000 for a single taxpayer or $183,000 for joint return taxpayers) always run a calculation to determine if making a Roth IRA contribution is appropriate. Also note that the Roth IRA income limits change from time to time, so always check the applicable income limits each tax year. As mentioned earlier, the Roth IRA is generally an excellent choice for those who expect to be in the same or a higher income tax bracket during retirement as they are today. Where the Roth IRA may not be as suitable is the case of a taxpayer in a high income tax bracket today who anticipates he or she will be in any substantially lower income tax bracket during retirement.

Roth 401(k)

The Roth 401(k) is a recent development that has tremendous impact and advantages for high income participants. As we have seen with the Roth IRA, there is an upper income limit that precludes most high income earners from contributing to a Roth IRA.

What is unique about the Roth 401(k) is the absence of an upper income limit; there is **no restriction** against making a contribution into a Roth 401(k). This is a tremendous benefit for high income earners who will presumably always be in a high tax bracket during both their working years and retirement. The Roth 401(k) allows these employees the opportunity to save a substantial amount of money upon which there will never be any income tax on the earnings.

Let us take a look at the example of Sarah Hightower who is a 50-year-old executive earning $250,000 per year. Due to her income Sarah cannot make a contribution to a Roth IRA but because her employer offers a Roth 401(k), (using the 2011 contributions limit of $16,500 plus the over age 50 "catch-up" provision of $5,500) she can contribute up to the maximum of $22,000 per year. Although the maximum 401(k) contribution will change over the years, let us use $22,000 for our contribution for the following calculations:

Sarah contributes $22,000 per year for 15 years for a total contribution of $330,000. Using a 5% compound interest assumption, the value 15 years from now when Sarah is 65 year old will be $498,465. Based upon a 5% income withdrawal rate, Sarah will be able to take $24,923 per year income tax free.

The advantage to Sarah of the Roth 401(k) is that she will have $24,923 per year that will not be taxable regardless of her other income and assets. Note that although the income is tax-free you must begin taking withdrawals from the Roth 401(k) once you reach age 70 ½. This is different from the Roth IRA wherein you do not have to begin taking withdrawals at age 70 ½.

Even if the investor buys US Government Bonds, the yield may generally be higher and the investor will get both an increased return and a tax-free return on the money initially contributed. This may be further enhanced by investing in equities (assuming that one can get a positive return in the equity markets!)

ACTION STEPS:

- High income bracket taxpayers should consider tax free municipal bonds for some portion of their fixed income assets.

- Use Roth IRA's and Roth 401(k)'s where you anticipate being in the same or higher income tax bracket in retirement as during your working years.

BOTTOM LINE

Keep saving into a retirement plan during downturns to accumulate capital and benefit from any employer match and dollar cost averaging.

Dollar Cost Averaging

A question that comes up during periods of uncertainty is: *Should I keep saving and investing?* The answer to that is emphatically, **Yes!** Although you may change the investments selected, there are two important reasons to continue to save and invest during turbulent markets.

The need for consistent systematic savings was discussed earlier. It is essential to save a portion from every paycheck. Even during periods where we are skeptical about the soundness of any investment, the basic need and importance of saving must be continued. If you are totally unsure as to where to put money, then use a savings account insured by the FDIC in a bank.

The other reason to continue saving is to take advantage of what is known as dollar cost averaging. Dollar cost averaging is a systematic process whereby a set dollar amount is invested periodically. Under this arrangement when prices are down the investor gets more shares. Dollar cost averaging does not nor cannot guarantee that you will make money. For dollar cost averaging to show a positive return, the markets must have a general upward trend during the accumulation period.

Here is an example of dollar cost averaging:

In this example we will assume that the investor is making a regular monthly purchase of Yugo Corporation Stock. The investor will purchase $100 worth of the stock each month.

In the first month, the share price is $20 per share. The investor buys $100 worth of the stock and at $20 a share buys five shares. (For simplicity, we have ignored transaction costs, but those should always be evaluated by the investor prior to making an investment)

During the second month, the share price dropped in half to $10. This means that the existing five shares purchased the first month are now worth only $50. Despite the drop the investor still buys $100 more of the stock. At $10 per share the investor gets 10 shares, so now has a total of 15 shares.

> *In the third month, the shares have risen to $25. The investor buys $100 worth of and receives four shares for a current total of 19 shares.*
>
> *In the fourth month the share price has returned to its original $20 per share. The 19 shares are now worth $380, the investor's cost basis is $300 so there is now has a gain of $80.*

As we said earlier, dollar cost averaging does not and cannot guarantee that the investor will make money. However dollar cost averaging especially when it is regular, systematic and automatic ensures that the investor buys through both good and bad times. This increases the likelihood that the investor will make at least some purchases in a down market and therefore get the benefit of purchasing at a lower price and getting more shares for the same dollar amount.

"Will We Ever See 6 Percent Again?" – Revisited

I previously introduced the reader to Woody Woodson in chapter 1. In the early 1980s he made an astute observation about the dramatic swing in interest rates during his lifetime. He compared the very low interest rates of the 1930s during the depression with the very high interest rates of the late 1970s and early 1980s. He described how twice in his lifetime he had heard the refrain, "Will we ever see 6% again?" By that he meant during the 1930s the question was would interest rates ever rise back up to 6% and in the 1980s would they ever drop below double-digit levels back to 6%. Here are his own words describing this event:

> *"In my own adult lifetime, I have twice heard the financial world cry out in agonized tones 'Do you suppose we will ever see 6%*

again?' I heard in the 1930s when savers and investors were hard-pressed to get more than 1.5% and I heard it in the late 1970s and early 1980s when borrowers and debtors were suffering from a going rate of 10% to 20% or even more. But I now venture the opinion that the long-term trend for interest rates is strongly downward, government deficits and inflation rates notwithstanding. I believe the pendulum will swing back. It always has." (Life Association News, April, 1983)

Mr. Woodson wrote those words in 1983 and as he predicted interest rates did indeed drop substantially. Now nearly 30 years later, to paraphrase Mr. Woodson, we once again hear the financial world cry out in agonized tones "will we ever see 6% again?" The pendulum has indeed swung back to a very low interest rate environment and if we look into the financial "crystal ball" it is plausible that in the ensuing decades the refrain will be heard again and again.

The point in all this is to emphasize that interest rates can and do fluctuate and that investors, savers and borrowers need to be aware of the dramatic impact that a shift in interest rates can create. It is especially important as you make your financial plans to take into account the dramatic impact that even a slight change in interest rates can have as you project your savings goals and your income needs during retirement. As you **do your planning,** use a variety of interest rates both high and low even if they seem unlikely at the time so that you have a concept of how fluctuations in interest rates will impact your portfolio and your retirement income; then err on the conservative side and use a lower interest assumption in your planning.

"Elvis Impersonators Predict Future Rates of Growth!"

No, that headline was not taken from a tabloid newspaper, but rather the cautionary tale of making growth assumptions based upon prior performance and experience. In 1977, the year Elvis Presley died, there were 234 Elvis impersonators making a living doing impressions of "The King". By the year 2000, there were 85,000 such impersonators. Using that rate of growth, by the year 2019, one prognosticator predicted that one-third of the world's population would be Elvis impersonators, far more presumably than demand. That line of reasoning demonstrates the fallacy in assuming that a given rate of growth will always remain constant. The point is that the rate of growth will almost never be constant and that returns will fluctuate as demand and market forces dictate.

So in your planning, use an assumed rate of growth or interest rate, but always run several rates and re-run the projections periodically and especially anytime there has been a dramatic downward shift in rates of return in the market.

CHAPTER 3

TAKE ACTION!

Jim Rohn's Advice

Elsewhere in this book, I referred to the book, *The Richest Man in Babylon* by George Clausen, the key point that the author makes is this little phrase "A part of all I earn is mine to keep". If you think about it, we all earn a paycheck; yet much of that paycheck, sometimes all or even more than all of that paycheck, is already committed. It goes to pay all of our bills. The key principle of savings you just saw in the circles is that you **must pay yourself first**. That is, you must save a part of all income, business revenue or wages that you make. The key is to develop a systematic, preferably automatic way to save on a regular basis.

I mentioned the Clausen book for two reasons. One, the importance of saving a part of all revenue and two, from a lesson learned from a man named Jim Rohn. In 1999, I attended an evening seminar where Jim was the featured speaker and he talked about the book, *The Richest Man in Babylon*. I had read a borrowed copy of the book perhaps ten years or more prior to hearing the speech so I was familiar with the book. Jim went on to extol the virtues of the information in this book and then he said something that I've always remembered. He said, "Now it's very easy to go out and buy the book and learn its lessons" but then he said, "It's also easy *not* to do it!" His point was that there are many things that we know we need to do, that are easy to do, and yet paradoxically are also easy not to do and so we never get around to doing them.

Right then and there I promised myself that the next morning I would go out and buy a copy of that book and indeed that very next day I went to a bookstore and bought two copies, one for myself and one to give to a colleague. So Jim's advice holds true for all of us. **Many things are easy to do and they are also easy not to do.** You will see later in this book a simple diagram that can help all of us to do the things we need to do in a timely manner.

BOTTOM LINE

Almost everyone struggles with procrastination. Make the desired result more powerful and compelling to overcome the inertia, and get started NOW!

Beating Procrastination

At a summer job I had while in college, Jack Sherman, a cagey old sales manager at the Chrysler garage used to ask the salespeople, "If you wish in one hand and you spit in the other hand, which hand will get full faster?"

He posed this crude question to illustrate the difference between wanting something and actually doing something about it. How often have you kicked yourself because you had a great goal or idea or dream or vision, yet after some time, had not made any progress? The difference between what we say we want to accomplish and what we actually do is called the **Implementation Gap**.

The closer you can get to the top line of goals, plans, dreams, and visions of the actions required, the more consistently you take steps toward success. The key is to **build habit, consistency, and repetition**, making as many aspects as possible automatic. That is why a payroll deduction into a retirement plan or an automatic transfer from your checking account to your savings account can be so powerful.

Andy Grove's Doodle

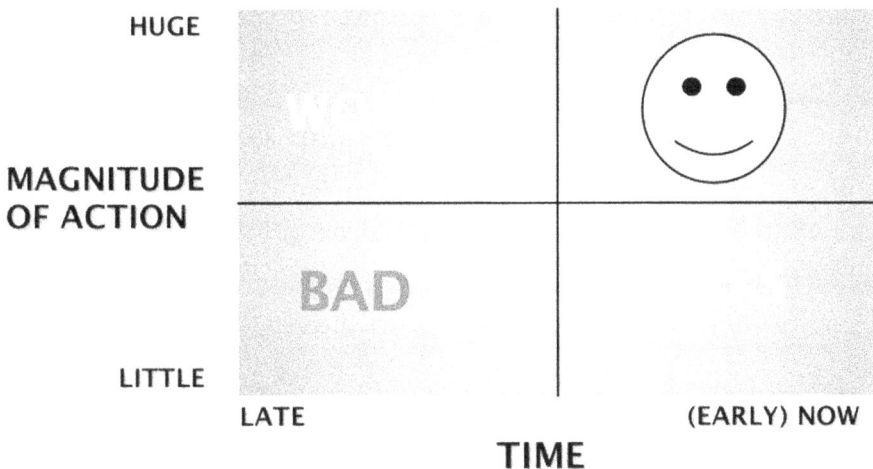

I have used a little doodle for years that I first spotted in an article in Fortune magazine interviewing Andy Grove, founder of Intel. As you can see from the chart, the twin pillars of "magnitude of action" combined with word "early" serve to get you to take a large amount of action immediately.

Here is how the chart works:

Think of your college days when you were assigned a term paper. If you worked on it early in the term, did the research, wrote the first draft, there was plenty of time to get it done and do it properly. Yet, how many millions of college students over the decades have pulled the "all-nighter", feverishly writing the term paper the night before it was due? The all-nighter is a perfect example of the quadrant that shows a huge amount of action done very late. As Mr. Grove's chart shows, it "works," but it is probably not your best effort.

The Olympic athlete who trains every day for years and then wins a medal has done both a huge amount of action and started the process early. The result is the medal in the upper right quadrant. The more frequently you use the principle behind Mr. Grove's little doodle, the more goals, plans, dreams and visions you can and will accomplish in your life.

An interesting aspect of this chart is how it relates to saving money. If you only put in a small amount, but you start "early" and you are consistent, the plan will "work." If you wait until very late, it takes a huge "Magnitude of Action" (in this case money) to make it "work," and of course the huge amount of money required to achieve the goal simply may not be possible.

Of course, if you can put a larger amount of money into savings and start early, then you can get to the happy face in the upper right quadrant.

BOTTOM LINE

Human nature is such that it is often easier to procrastinate than work on a "self-directed" goal or project. The key is to build a system that keeps one focused and on track.

ACTION STEPS

- Draw out this little doodle and put it where you can see it every day.

- Build accountability systems with friends and colleagues.

- Recognize both internal and external sources of encouragement.

"How's That Book Comin' Along?"

Procrastination can hamper us not only in our finances, but in many aspects of our lives.

But let us hold off on talking about procrastination because it's time for lunch... Off I go to Porter Street Barbeque. There are Theo and Joe cooking up a storm: tri-tip, chicken, the works. Right after I hear, "Do you want a half BBQ chicken with sauce?" the very next words are, "How's that book comin' along?" And now my "out to lunch" frame of mind is suddenly jolted back to my project. How IS that book coming along? Sometimes the answer would be that I had written another paragraph or edited a passage. Other times, the truth was that I hadn't done a darn thing (because I was busy or worried about a problem or some other "the dog ate my homework" excuse).

After having tucked into the barbecued chicken, it is now time for a snack. Off to the Smoothie Store. There Ralph starts my order and asks, "When will you have your book finished?"

It's 8:30 Monday morning. Time for the weekly conference call with my speaker study group, Beth, Trudy and Howard, "What progress did you make last week and what are your plans this week?"

This book you are now reading was something I wanted to do, not something that anyone made me do. It would have been easy enough (and it was at times) to not work on it or make any progress. But it was something I wanted to do and believed strongly that the ideas could be of great value to many people.

I was fortunate enough to have both a formal, structured support group, (my speaking study group), and an informal collection of people who knew about the project and encouraged me to finish it.

While I was working on the manuscript for this book, I told friends, colleagues, some clients and people that I would see on a regular basis about the project. I worked with my Speaker Group, Trudy Triner, Beth Proudfoot and Howard Miller during a once a month meeting and weekly conference calls. Each of us would update each other on our progress on speaking engagements, seminars, books and other projects. This group gave me (and continues to give) accountability and a motivation to work toward goals, in particular goals that are not "external", meaning from an employer or outside source, but rather from an "internal", self-directed goal.

A good method to help minimize or avoid procrastination, especially when a project is important but not immediately urgent, is to **build in some time frames and outside accountability**. One way to do this is to enlist friends, family and colleagues to follow up with you at specified time intervals to check on your progress.

Urgent Versus Important

Financially speaking, we have things we must do that are urgent, generally from an external source. We must pay our bills on time or the consequences will be dire; we must file our income tax return on April 15th each year, etc. The only "reward" for our effort is the absence of a negative result. Hardly inspirational!

Yet when it comes to things that are important but not urgent, we must build in that same sense of urgency. It is not "urgent" for you today to save money. Yet, the money you save today may prove to be extremely important if you lose your job three years from now, or want to retire a few years sooner, or have the money to send your daughter to medical school seven years from now or wish to leave a significant legacy to your favorite charity. **The reward for being pro-active with your financial affairs, now – today – can be very tangible and satisfying.**

With our financial lives, we must create a sense of urgency to begin to take action today, even though the dollars we are creating may not be used until decades in the future. Due to the truism that the first dollar in earns the most interest, the sooner we start and the more consistent we are in monitoring our situation, the greater are our chances for success.

Intention and Implementation

The key is to be clear about our intentions, our goals, dreams and aspirations and then to be consistent with implementation by making reasonable progress towards achieving our intentions.

ACTION STEPS

- Determine what it is for you that would make a huge difference in your life and that would give you satisfaction if you were to achieve it.

- Focus on how and what steps you need to achieve that objective.

- Enlist people who care about you in a way that builds in recurring accountability.

- Use the "Andy Grove Doodle" or similar reminder to stay on track.

"Failure to Proceed" - What to do in tough times

As every Rolls-Royce owner will attest, a Rolls-Royce never "breaks down" nor has any other sort of mechanical problem that can bedevil other makes of cars. However, Rolls-Royces can and do, from time to time, even with diligent and proper maintenance, suffer from that little idiosyncrasy known as a "Failure to Proceed." Such an event is always easily solved by a quick call to the auto club, followed by an emotional, teary-eyed wallet-emptying ceremony performed at a "Ye Olde British Car Repair Shoppe". Knowing that a Failure to Proceed can (and will!) happen, the prudent Rolls-Royce owner takes the following precautions:

- Buys a model that is statistically more reliable and buys a specific previously owned car that has a good, documented service history.

- Always performs the required preventative maintenance to avoid or minimize the chance of an FTP.

- Always has the cell phone, AAA card, fire extinguisher, tools, spare bottles of mineral oil for the brake and suspension systems, etc., in order to deal with a roadside calamity.

- Has an established relationship with a good mechanic and a network of "gear head" friends who have the cars themselves and can help troubleshoot.

- Always has enough money in the Swiss bank account (or tin can in the backyard) to perform the dreaded "wallet-emptying ceremony".

All the above can and does apply to your financial life. **The "Failure to Proceed" concept can be anything that happens to you financially.** It may be caused by your own missteps or may be caused by external forces beyond your control. Knowing that an FTP can (and will!) happen to you financially, the steps to take are parallel:

- Buy investment assets that are more likely to have success. For example, there is a vast difference between an FDIC-insured savings account in a bank and a speculative investment with an unscrupulous promoter.

- Monitor your investments to see if circumstances have changed and make adjustments as necessary.

- Have an "emergency kit" of savings and a back-up plan.

- Get good advice from competent professionals and qualified sources for advice on investments.

- Have an emergency fund. Replenish it in good times.

What to Do in Bad Times

The first thing to do in a difficult economy – Don't panic!

Whether it's caused by external forces, such as a drop in the stock market or real estate value, or by a personal crisis, like a job loss or serious illness of a family member, the first thing to do is not panic. It's okay to feel anxiety and okay to be worried and concerned about the future. Those emotions are real and there's no point in browbeating yourself for being worried, scared, anxious, frightened, and fearful of the future. But don't let those emotions carry you into panic-induced actions.

List the positives. After a bit of reflection, evaluate the positives, your strengths and the options that you have for dealing with the problem. The more you have done to prepare for whatever difficulty you face, the easier it will be to work through the problem. The person who has a relatively low debt structure can better withstand a job layoff.

The person who has saved money in several different kinds of savings vehicles, some in a long-term pension, some in easily accessible savings account, perhaps other assets in real estate and life-insurance collectibles or stocks, for example, the more options are available to get through the difficulty.

What you want to avoid is having to make a long-term sacrifice to solve a short-term problem. If your only source of money is a qualified retirement plan and you are under age 59½ and are forced to take money out of that plan to meet a mortgage payment or pay for a serious illness, for example, then you not only suffer the 10% tax penalty plus regular federal and state income taxes upon withdrawing that cash, you also lose the future growth that the account might have earned over the ensuing years. For example, if you have to take $10,000 out of a qualified retirement plan and you are under age 59 1/2, you will pay $1,000 in penalty, plus ordinary federal and state income taxes on the $10,000. If you are in a 30% combined federal and state income tax bracket that amounts to $3,000 in regular income tax, plus the $1,000 penalty for a total of $4,000 in taxes. This confiscatory amount is why most advisors discourage taking a withdrawal from a qualified retirement plan prior to age 59 1/2.

Reinvent Yourself...Again

Tough times often by necessity provide the stimulus for both employees and the self-employed to finally get around to acquiring new skills or adding new markets, products or services they had always thought of. Let us look at each situation separately.

Clean Out Your Desk!

Bette Southern was a corporate trainer for a major high tech firm. One day her firm was merged with another. A few days later, Bette and many of her co-workers were given 15 minutes to clean out their desks and were escorted out of the building to their cars by security guards. "Have A Nice Day!"

Consider the employee who has been laid off. Much of the immediate focus will be on trying to get a new job. To the extent possible during that job search, our employee should also take advantage of any job training programs available, either through the former employer's exit program or at a community college or other adult learning institution, or acquire a new skill or perhaps even look into a different industry where there may be better long-term opportunities.

All things being equal, prospective employers will choose new hires that have more skills and job experience. Good people skills come in handy also.

Occasionally the employee who finds himself suddenly out of work may decide that now is the time to finally start that business he's always promised himself. Generally this can be a good idea; however our fledgling business owner must ensure that he has enough capital to both start the business and live on a shoestring budget long enough for the business to become profitable. For a capital-intensive business, our new owner may have to "ramp up" over time. Some businesses are more suited than others to starting small and then growing. Do your research first.

Thank God I Paid Cash For The Rolls!

One of the best ways to research is to speak with others who have recently started businesses in the same or similar fields, analyze their experiences, and learn about the opportunities and pitfalls to watch out for. For the business owner who finds him or herself in an economic downturn, there are several steps to take. First, determine if the downturn is caused by the overall economy or if the drop in sales or revenue is specific to that industry.

If the drop in sales is due to general economic decline, then the key for our business owner is to continue to market and advertise rather than retrench, and to come up with better ways to keep customers and more unique marketing approaches to attract new customers.

If the drop in sales is industry-specific, then the business must begin to look to new product development, quality improvement, or some other area that can differentiate its products from its competitors.

If it simply turns out that our business owner makes a product for which the demand is permanently disappearing, for example buggy whips or typewriters, then the business owner needs to look to new products and services, which may be quite unrelated to the existing lines.

(Of course, in a few instances, there may still be a small niche market. Buggy whips and typewriters might be needed as props for movie sets. The maker of a product that is "disappearing" should at least explore a creative way to find a unique use or application for the now obsolete product. In the course of my travels, I have been on several short train lines that are no longer used for their intended purpose, such as mining, but because they pass through a scenic gorge or canyon they have been adapted to a spectacular tourist train that provides employment and generates revenue into the local economy).

Golden opportunity – Buy an ailing competitor. If you have saved your money and have well-established lines of credit, there may be an opportunity for you to expand during a downturn by acquiring a competitor who is going out of business. . Then when the economy comes back up, you'll be well-positioned for a healthy expansion.

Don't despair. Whether employed, self-employed, or unemployed, **don't let tough times make you give up**. It is always important to remember that economies do expand and contract, and although governments seek to regulate and provide safety nets to mitigate some of the volatility, the reality of capitalism is that some periods are simply going to be better than others. The key is to always remember at the top of the cycle that things won't always be rosy and perfect, and conversely to remember at the bottom of the trough that things won't always remain doom and gloom either.

"Make Hay While the Sun Shines" – What to do in good times

There is an old expression in farming that says: "Make hay while the sun shines." This wise admonition pointed out to farmers of old that the alfalfa needed to be harvested, dried, and bailed into hay before the rains came. And so it is with our financial lives. We have windows of opportunity in which we can create something, and it must be done on a timely basis. Additionally, money, like the harvest, must be stored and gathered into the barn for use during the long hard winter that is sure to follow.

Our financial lives, however, do not always follow the exact predictability of the seasons. For some people, financial winter seldom, if ever, comes to them, or if it does, it's very mild and very brief, whilst others always seem to be shoveling snow. We cannot control external factors, such as how the global markets are performing, but we can recognize that fortunes ebb and flow, and that we do have some power to anticipate and either prevent or minimize negative economic circumstances.

So in good times when money is flush and it feels like the value of one's home, one's portfolio, one's collectibles, one's real estate, one's everything is on the march inexorably upward, that is the time to "make hay while the sun shines" – to build or fortify a solid financial foundation.

Here are two essential things to do during extraordinarily good times:

- Increase your level of savings from the basic recommendation of 10 percent of your income to 15 percent or even 20 percent.

- Pay off debt, or at least pay down debt. If you can't do that, at the very least, restructure debt at better terms with lower interest rates. Then if things take a turn for the worse, the debt structure is more manageable as to the amount, terms or the interest rate.

Often in good times there is the temptation to go out and buy all those goodies that you deferred buying during leaner years. It's okay to splurge and enjoy the fruits of your labor; that's what we work for. But don't go overboard; keep your goals in mind and stay focused. Here is where the concept of paying cash for the luxuries of life makes sense. Doing so forces you to buy only those things you truly can afford so you will not be stuck with a fancy car or boat or other trinket that you'll have to sell at a loss during a down period because you are over-leveraged.

Debt: Eliminate, Reduce, Restructure

Good times normally present an excellent opportunity to reduce or eliminate debt. Periods in which one's salary has risen or business revenue is higher than usual provide the additional cash to pay down debt.

For those on a salary or fixed income, the strategy is to pay a larger amount on the account with the smallest balance first. Say, for example, you have one credit card with a $5,000 balance, a second with $2,000 owed, and a third with $1,000. (We will assume that the interest rates on all three accounts are similar.) You would make the required minimum payments on the two larger accounts and pay an additional amount on the smallest account. The goal here is to get the $1,000 account balance paid off. Once that is done, you only have two accounts to make payments on, and all of the cash flow that was devoted to paying on the $1,000 account may now be applied to the $2,000 account and so on.

A variation of this strategy may occur if one of the three accounts in our example has a substantially higher interest rate than the other two. Using our previous example, let us say for argument's sake that the $2000 account balance had a 10% interest rate while the other two accounts were at 6%. In this scenario you would apply the extra payment on the $2000 account first. That reduces the account with the highest interest expense first and has the greatest impact in reducing your overall interest cost.

In all these examples, as in every case, it is vital to always make at least the minimum payment on every account on time in order to preserve one's good credit.

The final debt-reduction strategy during good times is to take advantage of opportunities to restructure debt. This may be particularly true for one's home mortgage if interest rates have dropped and the overall costs of refinancing can be offset by a lower future interest rate.

It is important to remember, however, that a lower payment may not necessarily be a better long-range value. If your payment goes down by the percentage rate of the interest paid on the loan and/or the number of years is higher for the aggregate total interest that would be paid on the loan is held to maturity, then it may not make sense to refinance. Always compare the total interest you will pay under any current loan against the total interest that would be paid to maturity on any proposed arrangement. Most states require that the lender provide the borrower with a statement which clearly indicates the percentage rate and the aggregate (total) amount of interest you will pay if you hold the loan to maturity and pay as per the schedule. Always compare the aggregate interest cost (and loan fees and costs) of the proposed loan against the remaining aggregate interest cost of the existing loan. Then factor in how long you are going to own the house. That will help you determine which path to take.

The key in all cases is that if you are maintaining your good credit and if you have relatively low amounts of debt, it will perhaps be easier to find and arrange for good terms.

We will review the advisability of borrowing on one's 401(k) in Chapter 6.

Reinvent Yourself

Another area to focus on during good times is improving one's own personal skills and marketability as an employee or, if self-employed, developing new markets, product lines or services that can be added to your business.

Frequently, as we'll discuss during the bad times scenario, a person who gets laid off – or a business owner whose customer base dries up – will be jolted into taking action when necessity becomes the mother of invention. In some ways it is more difficult to expand or add a new skill when times are good and the wolf is not at the door because the sense of urgency is not present. Seeing the cyclical nature of the economy, however – as recent events have proven – helps us recognize and elevate to a sense of urgency the need for self-improvement and take advantage of the good times to prepare for future downturns.

Rob Taylor, a long-time friend and a real prince of a guy, is both a business owner and a representative for a fuel jobber. He started with a firm owned by his father and later became its president. Several years ago it became apparent that it made sense to sell to a larger firm. A fuel jobber the size of his father's company or his father's predecessor simply could not exist today. The major fuel companies want, and economics dictate, a certain minimum volume. Although today he is gainfully employed, his industry has experienced and will continue to experience consolidation.

Although he has a good job, Rob went back to school for his master's degree in business administration. The price tag was about $16,000. Rob was able to make that investment whilst gainfully employed. How likely would it be for Rob if he became unemployed to spring for sixteen grand? Not very!

A few years later, Rob was offered a chance to buy a gourmet chocolate company, Stafford's Famous Chocolates. Its founder had died a few years previously and the family wanted to sell. Rob's years of real world experience combined with his MBA prepared him for the opportunity. The moral of this story is: **prepare**

yourself when you have the opportunity, or in other words, make hay while the sun shines!

As an employee who has a good job with an employer that appears to be solid and with good future employment prospects, you have opportunities to acquire new skills and education that may prove useful under one of these four scenarios:

Your new skills and training may qualify you for promotion or advancement within your current firm.

If you find that there is no room or possibility for advancement in your present firm, your new skills, combined with your previous experience, may qualify you for a better position with another company.

If your present employer should run into a hard patch and lay off people or, heaven forbid, close its doors, your new skills and education will leave you in a better position to compete for a job elsewhere.

Your skills and experience may mean that you can become self employed and run your own company, or partner with others.

Perhaps you would like to get into a totally different field unrelated to your current job. During good times, although you may be able to attend school on a part-time basis in order to meet the demands of your job, your current income can fund the required education or training to develop your new career without incurring tens of thousands of dollars in debt for school loans.

This can make an extended course of schooling affordable and feasible, easing your transition to a more desirable or suitable situation.

Now let us consider the self-employed person. We will assume that our business owner is reasonably successful and is earning a profit. Without being overly pessimistic, it is important for our successful business owner to ask herself what if the product or service that she sells or makes or offers is no longer desired by her customers? What if the economy changes? What if another supplier can provide the same thing for lower cost?

During good times a business owner should always be looking for ways to strengthen relations with existing customers, add complementary product lines and services, and expand her customer base. How can she add new markets, either geographically or by adding customers within her existing service area? Are there additional products and services that her existing customers might also buy? Does she have, or can she establish, a database of current customers that will help her understand both how to market to existing customers for repeat business and how to attract new customers?

Developing new product lines diversifies the business, helping protect it in the event that the demand for the current products and services diminishes. The key here is that business owners must simultaneously focus on core competencies and basic bread-and-butter business while expanding their customer bases and adding new product lines or services.

Business owners too often make drastic changes or finally begin innovating only during bad times when it literally is "sink or swim." The business owner who can solidify, diversify and expand during good times, with the support of positive cash flow and earnings, will be able to do so much more effectively.

"Who wants to be a millionaire?"

A few years ago a TV quiz show with the above title was the hottest ticket on television. It later became an integral part of the plot of the Academy Award winning movie "Slumdog Millionaire". Small wonder. Deep down, who really doesn't want to be a millionaire? Although as we have discussed, money is not the end-all and be-all of life, (in the movie, the hero appears on the show to help him find his lost love rather than win the money), the reality is that in a capitalist society a certain amount of capital is truly required to have a reasonable standard of living.

Sometimes, frankly, it's a bit frightening if we really examine just what $1,000,000 will actually do for us. If you have $1 million in a hypothetical investment account that is paying 5% per year, it will generate $50,000 per year in income. Although $50,000 is a respectable sum, it would not provide enough income for someone who was living on it to consider themselves as being "rich". Yet technically as a millionaire most people would probably consider themselves as being wealthy.

BOTTOM LINE

Systematic savings over a long period of time
can amount to a substantial sum.

The tougher issue about becoming a millionaire is that many Americans will never achieve a net worth of one million dollars.

So then how do we create $1 million? The old joke is that there are two ways to make $1 million; either marry it or inherit it. We will assume for the sake of discussion that neither option is available to our reader. Here is the third option:

We must quite simply save a certain amount every month based on the chart.

MILLIONAIRE CHART

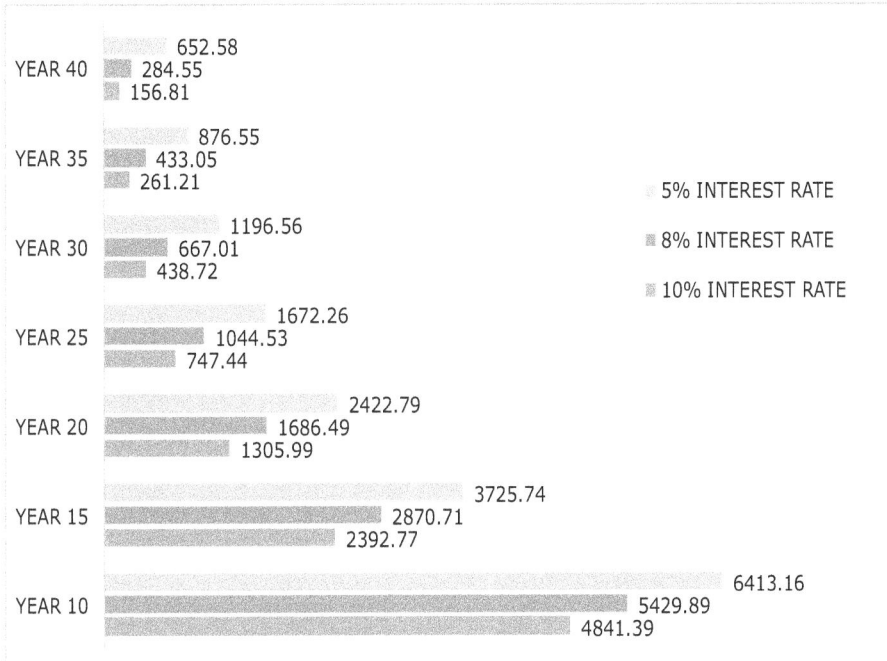

YEAR 40
652.58
284.55
156.81

YEAR 35
876.55
433.05
261.21

YEAR 30
1196.56
667.01
438.72

YEAR 25
1672.26
1044.53
747.44

YEAR 20
2422.79
1686.49
1305.99

YEAR 15
3725.74
2870.71
2392.77

YEAR 10
6413.16
5429.89
4841.39

5% INTEREST RATE
8% INTEREST RATE
10% INTEREST RATE

Let me preface this chart with a caveat about rates of return. The chart assumes that a hypothetical investment will earn a set rate of return for the entire period. The reality is that few investments ever make a set return year in and year out, especially over long periods of time. Even the rates of return on money market, certificates of deposits and bank passbook savings accounts will change as future interest rates change. (The exception would be a long-term bond whose interest rate remains constant for the life of the bond. The rate on a bond issued in 2010 by a company will be different than the rate offered by that some company on a new bond issued in subsequent years) The idea of this chart is to help you get a ballpark idea of how much savings it takes over a certain period of time to reach $1,000,000.

A 25-year-old at 8% interest needs $284 a month or roughly a little under $10 a day. Now if we can get 10% it only takes $156 a month or just a little over five dollars a day and our 25-year-old can have $1 million by age 65.

Imagine that you're 40 years old and you want to have $1 million when you are age 65; that's 25 years from now. If you look at our column under 25 years, you can see that at 8% you need to save $1,044 every month at 8%; if you do that, our 40 year old will have $1 million at age 65.

Now in the real world, people's savings amounts will vary from month to month, year to year, as their income and circumstances change; the point is to begin the discipline of saving systematically.

The key point the chart illustrates is that if a person will start out at an early age, ideally in their 20s, even a modest sum of money consistently invested each month in an account over a 30, 35 or 40 year period can accumulate, with earnings, to $1,000,000.

ACTION STEPS:

- Begin today, no matter how modest, to save a part of each paycheck.

- Recognize that no investment ever makes the same rate of return year after year over a long period of time. Increase your savings rate as needed if rates of return decline.

- Monitor your investments. Reallocate based upon your then current goals and objectives.

When to take chips off the table

The concept of when to take the chips off the table from your investments depends on several factors. They are:

- Potential for the investment to continue to grow

- Possibility that the investment growth curve may have peaked or flattened or potentially will decline

- "Panic"

- Alternative use for the money

- Tax implications

- In some instances, sentimental or emotional attachment

Growth Potential

The first area to evaluate in an investment that one is considering selling all or part of is whether that investment is likely to continue to grow. In this case we will assume that we bought or inherited the assets and that it has grown at a reasonable or maybe a very good rate during the period we have held it. The question then becomes is that growth rate likely to continue or has the investment peaked? Often with a stock, the investor or the investors adviser will set a target range at the outset of the purchase that they hoped to achieve and then once the stock has reached that point, begin to sell off all or part of that position.

BOTTOM LINE

Plan for the fun things in life. You can enjoy life along the way and not break the bank.

Growth Peaked or Declining

The next area to consider is whether the investment has reached its zenith from a growth perspective. Will the rate of growth going forward be relatively slow or has the asset peaked? We might have a small-cap stock that has been a growth stock that we've held for several years where the company or the industry in which the company is based has now become a more mature industry and after a period of spectacular growth it may now offer much more modest growth.

A further consideration is if the industry has peaked or is in the doldrums and is not likely to recover in the near term.

"Panic"

One of the key times when an investor will "evaluate" whether to take chips off the table is during periods of panic. Whenever the computer screen is flashing red and every newscast has a prophesy of doom and gloom, even the most seasoned investors may struggle with the word "evaluate" and allow emotions to overrule their judgment.

The key in times of panic, as we said earlier, is to take a deep breath and reevaluate whether the investment is still fundamentally sound, that is whether the stock or a piece of real estate still has intrinsic value that over time can recover value or whether in fact the value will continue to plummet and one should minimize the losses and cut and run. The key is to make these evaluations in as clear-eyed a manner as possible and filter through the bad news and hysteria and determine how much is valid and how much is hype. In some cases it will not be possible to accurately determine whether there is a potential for a particular investment to recover.

The key about panic times is that **if we have built the base of safety, there is less need to panic** and a lower likelihood that cash flow or other circumstances require you to bail out at a bad time.

Alternative Uses

The next consideration is what you want to do with the proceeds if the asset is sold. Frequently a new opportunity will trigger the idea about selling an existing asset. So there may be an opportunity to buy a stock that has good growth potential or a piece of real estate that is available at a good value with what you believe has a good upside potential. First you evaluate the potential growth and income of each investment. Secondly, you have to weigh the cost (taxes, fees, etc) of getting out of the old investment with the opportunity of getting into the new investment.

Income Tax Considerations

For the discussion about tax consideration we must divide the asset class into qualified retirement plan assets versus real estate investment versus most other assets. We will consider each category separately.

For qualified plan monies the good news is that generally speaking as long as the monies remain within the umbrella of the qualified plan there is no tax consideration between moving from one investment to another, as long as the funds remain in a tax qualified plan. The benefit of a qualified plan, and one of the key reasons that we recommend them for most people, is that investment changes can be made without having to consider the tax implication. For investors with substantial qualified plan assets we are now often seeing people with six and even seven figures in their qualified plans; this can provide a tremendous amount of flexibility.

A key reason for even a wealthy, sophisticated investor to use a qualified retirement plan is in fact this very ability to make investment changes within the qualified plan without having to recognize current income tax. So if the investor anticipates making a fair number of trades within an account, he or she should investigate using qualified plan monies for the more actively traded account. Augment the qualified retirement plan with a non-qualified account where the investor uses a buy-and-hold strategy with less frequent trading.

(I do not recommend that clients "day trade" within a retirement account).

For the investor who holds a piece of real estate it may be possible to initiate a 1031 exchange by buying a qualifying property of equal or greater value. The benefit here is that with a 1031 exchange the investor does not recognize capital gain tax currently. For example, an investor may have owned a single-family home that was used as a rental property and does a 1031 exchange to a property with multiple units with the idea that the new building will provide more income for the investor. If properly done this might be an appropriate change and offer the required income. Care should always be used with any 1031 exchange and the advice of a qualified CPA or tax attorney and title company should be sought to ensure the transaction is done correctly and will meet the standards set forth by the IRS.

Finally, for what we might call portfolio accounts (that is stocks, bonds, collectibles, anything you own where when you sell it you have to pay either regular income tax or capital gains tax), then the tax implications do need to be factored into making a decision about selling or retaining an asset. The calculation that should be performed is to estimate the after-tax amount of money and then compare the growth of after-tax money in whatever the proposed new investment is and compare that with simply leaving the asset in its current position.

Of course, if you have determined that the existing asset has reached its peak performance or has the potential to be diminished in value and conversely the proposed asset has a good chance of growth, then it will make sense in that case to take chips off the table, pay the tax and re-invest in the new asset.

The other place where cashing in may make sense is where the management of a particular asset is now onerous or burdensome to the investor. The classic case is the investor who owns a piece of rental property and either due to age or circumstance has grown tired of the effort to maintain and manage the property. In this case that sole factor may loom large enough that it makes sense to sell, even with a tax bite. In addition to the hard facts such as the tax implications there may also be the emotional or lifestyle factor of reducing one's stress.

Another area where taking chips off the table may be appropriate is due to the investor's age where a more aggressive investment is no longer suitable for his or her time horizon and the investor wishes to have the assets in a more conservative investment. A classic example of this would be a growth stock where the investor now wishes over time to move those monies to a municipal bond to provide both more stability and a tax-free income.

Sentimental Journey

Finally, in some cases an investor may hold an asset that has a sentimental or emotional value. This often occurs where the asset is an inherited item. It may be a home or land or even stock that one's parent or grandparent owned for many, many years. It may be a collectible piece of art or other asset that has a sentimental or evocative attachment.

There are no right or wrong answers in terms of keeping a sentimental asset. What is always important to be aware of if there is a sentimental factor and that if one chooses to keep an asset, even one whose return or growth potential is limited, that if one chooses to keep the asset due to its sentimental value then as long as one has the ability to meet their obligations and achieve their desired lifestyle and understands that one is keeping an underperforming asset for sentimental reasons then that's okay. This is one of the reasons why we encourage people to have numerous buckets of assets so that there is room to have the sentimental asset.

CHAPTER 4

DEBT/SPENDING

Grandmother's New Buick

Most people today when they wish to buy a major, big-ticket item will whip out their credit card and charge it. But it wasn't always that way. Let's return for a moment to yesteryear. Let me tell you about my grandmother's new Buick. My grandparents lived all their working lives on my grandfather's salary as a civil engineer. When they retired to the family ranch in 1947, they had a modest pension and a small amount of Social Security, yet every eight years, over a span of almost 30 years, they bought a brand-new Buick for cash. How did they do that on a small retirement income? Simple enough, they saved their money year after year so that in 1950 they bought the 1950 Buick Road-master. Then for the next eight years they saved their money so that by 1958 with the money they had saved, plus the trade-in, they could buy the 1958 Buick Special with cash. I remember that car with its huge chrome fins and a ribbon style speedom-eter that was fascinating to watch as a young child. Eight years later, again with proper savings and a trade-in, they bought the 1966 Buick Wildcat and it was fast! As a post-script to this story, there was no 1974 Buick LeSabre as Granddaddy had passed away a few years earlier and Grandmother stopped driving; however, Grandmother did have more than enough saved to buy a new car in 1974 had she still needed one.

The point is that even though their income was modest, **they saved toward a goal**. They let compound interest work for them rather than paying interest that they would have had to on a car loan. The difference is they had to wait a few years before the next car but by waiting a few years they always had something nice and wonderful. And most importantly, Granddaddy could sit in the car with his hat on!

You and I can use that same "virtual layaway" plan ourselves. Rather than charge or borrow and pay interest, delay making the purchase for that special item, until you have the cash. It may take a few months or maybe even a few years, but when you save your money even in a simple bank account or in a Certificate of Deposit, you have interest work for you rather than paying interest on a credit card. It means that when the time comes to buy the item you have the cash. It may mean that you can take advantage if there is a sale or a special offer. It means that no matter what your circumstances are or your standard of living, you can have something at a better value than the person who is dependent on their credit card, since interest helps you buy the item, rather than loan interest adding to the purchase price!

5% Fun Spending Rule

The 5% fun spending rule is designed to help you balance savings and necessities with enjoying life along the way. It serves as a guide as to how much to spend for things that are not necessities. The concept is that no more than 5% of income is spent on things that are "nice to have" but are not an absolute necessity.

SAVING FOR A CAR VERSUS A CAR LOAN

SAVING FOR A CAR
THE TOTAL SAVINGS AMOUNT THAT A PERSON WHO SAVES UP FOR THE CAR IS $17,645.45 (THE REST IN INTEREST).

CAR LOAN
THE TOTAL THAT THE CAR LOAN PERSON PAYS IS $22,654.00, WITH A DIFFERENCE OF $5000 FROM THE PERSON SAVING FOR A CAR.

YEAR	TOTAL ANNUAL PAYMENTS	TOTAL INTEREST	ENDING BALANCE
			$20,000
1	$4,529	$918	$16,389
2	$4,529	$733	$12,593
3	$4,529	$539	$8,603
4	$4,529	$335	$4,409
5	$4,529	$120	$0

TWO PEOPLE COULD BUY THE SAME CAR FOR $20,000 AND THE SAVER PAYS $5,000 LESS (WHICH IS 25% FOR THE PRICE OF THE CAR) THAN THE PERSON TAKING OUT A CAR LOAN.

Someone earning $50,000 could spend up to $2,500 per year using that system. In this example, perhaps $1,000 for a nice home entertainment system is appropriate, but not one costing $10,000. Having a benchmark to operate within can help you prioritize. If you have two or three "goodies" on your wish list, and they cost more than the budget allows, you have to decide which item to get now and which to save for next year.

Of course, the 5% number is a guide. For someone unemployed, that number will be non-existent. A higher wage earner may be able to expand that number, but do so only with a corresponding increase in savings. We have seen that good years can turn to lean years, so enjoy, but save and plan for the future. If you find yourself spending 2% per year more on strictly fun items, increase your savings by 2% as well.

The further benefit of having a "fun" category in your budget is that you can enjoy those purchases and not feel guilty, because you have saved first and only spent a pre-determined amount. Life is a balance.

ACTION STEPS:

- Determine your "fun" budget. Use 5% of income as a starting point and adjust up or down as appropriate.

- Prioritize the "goodie" list so you can get the "Goodest Goodie" first!

Programmed Seepage and Needless Enrichment - The Dastardly Dynamic Duo

There are two insidious forces that work against you and me in our effort to achieve financial security: "Programmed Seepage" and "Needless Enrichment". Strictly speaking, "Programmed Seepage" is a British automotive term. It is a more polite way to say "oil leak". 'Programmed Seepage' somehow conveys the idea that the car is supposed to leave a puddle all over the garage floor! It's usage in financial terms means money that seems to sprout legs and run from your wallet or bank account. It is often for minor or frivolous items, but it may also be for something more substantial. Your goal financially is to minimize the incidents of such occurrences where practical and possible.

Sometimes programmed seepage occurs at sporadic intervals and other times it occurs in a methodical, planned way. Part of managing your finances is to evaluate all the things you spend automatically each month, such as your cellular telephone service, your cable service, etc. From time to time re-visit these "automatic" bills and make certain that you both need and use the service provided and then compare to see if you are getting the best value. If you find that you are not using something, then discontinue it (making certain to pay attention to any "exit" fees a company might charge).

"Needless Enrichment" describes any item or service that costs more than its intrinsic worth or value. This is particularly true where the person or company getting the needless enrichment has an unfair advantage and is in a position to dictate the terms and you have no choice. This can be for an item of any cost or dollar amount.

For example, something that is worth $1.00 for which the charge is $2.00 is needless enrichment, even though the extra dollar is very small in absolute terms. However, this is exactly the sort of thing that we want to avoid, because small amounts, extracted consistently over time will add up to a large amount.

In America today, there is often a great debate about how much a company might charge for a service, such as the fees on an ATM or debit card or the $25 per bag that some airlines charge. There are two sides of the equation that are equally true. A company may charge as much as the market will bear and/or regulations will allow. In a capitalist society, that is legally acceptable. The opposite is also true that we as consumers are not (or at least should not be) obligated to do business with a firm or company that overcharges or does not provide value equal to price charged. The exception of course is that there are circumstances where there is only one provider of a product or service or you have an emergency and you are stuck. The further issue is that some products or services may have hidden fees or "add-ons" that appear after you have committed to buying something. In some cases, you cannot easily determine the fees.

The due diligence that each of us must undertake is to structure our financial lives in a way that reduces, or ideally, eliminates the incidents of needless enrichment. It can mean that one does not do business with a firm or even an entire industry. Such a choice may mean a trade-off, but it is the only viable way that you and I as individuals can make a difference in how businesses operate. Where you know that you are faced with a needless enrichment scenario and can't avoid it, then do what is realistic to minimize it.

For example, use only a carry-on bag if you can possibly manage on air travel, or at the least, only one checked bag. I personally never shop for anything on a trip involving air travel, so I don't have extra "stuff" to schlep and pay for to get home. Does that mean that I occasionally pass by some souvenir or trinket that might be nice or fun to have? Yes. Does that mean that some merchant somewhere makes one less sale? Yes. Does it mean that I save the extra $25 fee to check this widget on an airplane? Yes. For me that is a worthwhile trade-off.

Adam Smith's "invisible hand" can be used by you and me in a small way to influence economic forces.

Feast or Famine – Cash flow management for the self-employed

Many financial planning guides are based upon a person or couple who are on a fixed salary or income stream, where the amount of income each month is a known quantity. The planning then revolves around making choices about allocating money, saving, paying down debt, investing, managing purchases, etc.

But very little advice or help is offered for the self-employed person who "enjoys" a fluctuating income. Some self-employed people are in a seasonal business or a cyclical business where cash flows vary from month to month. Some can fairly accurately predict the ebb and flow; others have less predictability.

The short answer to the problem is in four key areas:

1. Save money during good months

2. Have great credit and credit lines

3. Develop fixed and variable cost budgets

4. Build recurring revenue

Now let us look at these areas and develop some strategies to achieve each objective:

I. SAVE YOUR MONEY!!!

The key to all cash flow management is systematically saving a part of your revenue. There is a great line from the book, "The Richest Man in Babylon" by George Clauson, which states, "A part of all I earn is mine to keep". Make that idea a part of your business practice and save a part of each source of revenue. Set aside either a fixed dollar amount or a fixed percentage, or a graduated percentage. That way in a poor month, at least a small amount is saved and in a banner month or quarter, a substantial amount is saved.

What do we mean by "saved"? **Savings is defined here as any money put into an account and not used for current expenses**. These are dollars that you will use in the future. They may be readily accessible in a money market account or passbook savings, or they may be less accessible in a retirement plan (IRA, 401(k), time deposit, real estate, and stocks, bonds, or a cash value life insurance policy. In a perfect world, you will fund some of both liquid and less liquid savings vehicles.

Saving will do three things for the self-employed person. One, he or she will enjoy have the dollars sitting in an account, or better still, several accounts. This improves your balance sheet and strengthens your position to get credit and at better terms.

Two, there is the psychological benefit of having an account with money in it, with your name on it. The self-employed may find themselves in a position of having to "push on" during a lean time. There can be great comfort in knowing that you have a reserve and that it is not all for naught.

Three, you may be able to take advantage of an opportunity that can impact your business that requires cash. You might be able to buy useable inventory or raw materials at a sharp discount, if you have the cash. Perhaps you can expand your business or hire key talent. Having stability gives you the ability to take advantage of unique opportunities.

2. HAVE GREAT CREDIT AND CREDIT LINES

Credit is and has always been a double-edged sword. Like a powerful drug, the right amount can cure, but too much can kill. In fact the word "mortgage" is from the French word "mortir" which literally means, "to die".

On a positive side, credit can be used for opportunity and many entrepreneurs have made fortunes using leverage or credit. As a self-employed person, you must understand credit and manage it carefully so that it is the servant (and not the master!)

The first step, as simple as it sounds, is always **pay on time**. Even if it is only the minimum, pay on time. Did I mention that it is important to pay on time? Paying on time avoids having any unpleasant conversations with your creditors and generally gives you lower interest rates on most loans. It allows you to maintain credit lines and credit cards. These can be invaluable for getting through a lean period. It may mean that you can take advantage of an opportunity that will make a return in your business, even when business is slow and it isn't the "right time" in the short run, but will pay dividends in the long run.

As with savings, there is the psychological benefit of knowing that you are a responsible businessperson. You may not like the amount of the balance owed (no one does), but by paying on time you keep the wolf away from the door. Reducing your anxiety over debt by paying promptly allows you to focus on the task of increasing your revenue, which will make it easier to pay off debt.

There are two classic approaches to reducing debt. Let us look at a person with three accounts, one of $50,000, one for $3,500 and a third for $15,000. Let us look at the traditional strategy:

The first step is to concentrate on the smallest account balance first. That is, you pay the required minimum on the $50,000 and $15,000 loan, but pay more than the minimum on the $3,500. The idea here is to pay it off as soon as possible. For example, if a large amount of revenue comes in and you can meet all your other current expenses, you pay off the loan of $3,500. Now you are left with just two loans and you now have freed the money that was required for the $3,500 loan. You can now take that amount and increase the regular payment on the $15,000 loan.

You repeat this process until your loans are paid off.

The other option is a modification of the first idea. Here, you pay the minimum required payment on all your loans, except the one with the highest interest rate. On the loan with the highest rate, you pay as much additional amount as cash flow allows. This pays off the most expensive loan first. (Some business loans or lines may have a pre-payment limit that restricts pre-payment, so check the terms of your loan first. If you cannot pre-pay as much as you have available, then pre-pay on the next highest interest rate loan). You then proceed to the next highest interest rate loan. You may also be able to transfer balances to lower rate credit cards or credit lines, since you have been maintaining a good credit rating.

Your goal is to minimize your interest expense. Then, during lean months, you can borrow at favorable rates to keep going. You will have both the availability of credit and hopefully not at loan shark prices.

When you combine good savings habits with consistent attention to your credit, you strengthen the asset side of your net worth, while managing and reducing the liability side. As we have said several times, not only do you reap the monetary rewards, but gain the peace of mind factor that may just as valuable, if not more so.

3. BUDGET FOR FIXED COSTS AND VARIABLE COSTS

Budget!

For the self-employed, the budget consists of four areas:

Personal Budget
Fixed Expenses
Business Budget
Variable Expenses

Determine first those areas that are fixed such as mortgage payments, rents, and fixed loan payments. Analyze variable costs, such as utilities that fluctuate with the seasons, materials or inventory that change with workflows.

Now, determine a base level of savings, either a dollar amount or percentage. Then, structure a step-up or increase once you reach a certain level.

For example, you plan to save 5% of income up to the first $5,000 a month in revenue, but 10% on amounts above $5,000. The idea is that once you have covered your fixed costs, as revenue increases, a greater portion of each additional dollar of revenue can be allocated to either increased savings or reducing debt or a combination of both.

4. DEVELOP RECURRING REVENUE STREAMS

Evaluate your business and your industry to determine what opportunities exist to develop on-going revenue streams. One of the great problems of the self-employed is that revenue may come in only upon completion of a major job or project and then nothing in between. For example, a real estate broker and a mortgage broker generate revenue only when a sale closes escrow. The contractor who built the house or did the re-model gets paid when the job is completed. For people in these kinds of industries, it is critical to have an on-going stream of new business getting "into the pipeline". So while you are completing the current big job, you are also getting next month's (and next year's) business started.

Some businesses do lend themselves to recurring revenue. For example, a restaurant might have a frequent diner's club with discounts or specials. That will give the restaurant increased patronage and they will be able to better plan for food and staffing. Bookstores may send a discount coupon via e-mail to regular customers. This builds additional traffic into the store.

Search for ways to build recurring revenue that can be done for relatively low cost and low effort so that you can concentrate on your main business focus. The on-going revenue can be useful in building cash flow.

Thank God I Paid Cash For The Rolls!

A second, non-business strategy is to build an investment portfolio that can generate some current cash flow. The idea here is to have a source of income that can be used for expenses in a lean month and re-invested in good months. An investment portfolio might include bonds that pay interest, stocks that pay dividends or rental property that earns rental income. The key is to have investments that fit your time and the ability to manage so that you can focus on your primary business. No one type is best for all people.

SUMMARY

Using these four strategies can help the self-employed person manage the impact of fluctuations in cash flow. Improvement in one area will help other areas. The key is to work from a plan and make systematic progress.

A Tale of Two Houses

Jack and Nancy Vintner bought a house at the height of the overheated real estate market in a medium-sized city, Vineyard Valley, California. They took out a 10 year interest only loan with the idea that they would either sell the house within 10 years, or be able to re-finance (since house prices always go up, right?). They have good credit and always make the payment on time.

Yet a year and a half before the adjustable rate mortgage is set to "re-adjust", they find the value of the house has dropped and they cannot re-finance. The result will be that they will not be able to make the payments when the rate goes up. Nancy said "We are 60 years old and may lose our house and everything we have worked for, even with good credit and jobs."

78

So what can they do?

ACTION STEPS:

- In the case of Jack and Nancy, they could find a hard money lender to give them a small second mortgage to get to the right loan to value ratio.

- If possible, begin to save some money in an account to help cover the shortfall. This may help them buy time for the house to appreciate and later re-finance.

- If possible, pay down enough on the principal so that the loan to value ratio will meet a lender's requirement. This is usually 80/20%; that is, most lenders will not lend more than 80% of the property's appraised value.

* * *

- When purchasing a house, get a 30 or 15 year fixed mortgage, rather than an adjustable rate mortgage.

- If you can only get an adjustable rate mortgage, get a long guaranteed period, such as 10 years. That gives you more time to qualify for a fixed rate and time for the possibility that the value of the property will increase.

- Never assume that a property will appreciate. Ask yourself, "What if the value declines?"

- If you have an interest only mortgage (where no money is applied to reduce the principal), then either make a plan to pay some on the principal, or set up a separate account, known as a "sinking fund" so that you have some money available to either reduce the principal at a later point, or to help make a larger payment if the interest rate adjusts upward and you are not able to re-finance.

- Work with your lender for a loan modification if such an option is available. These can be difficult to get.

- Do your utmost to keep your credit score high. This gives you more options than someone with a low score.

The Other Side:

Kelly was a sales representative for an electrical manufacturer in 1977. As part of his compensation package, his employer gave him a $700 per month car allowance since he had a large territory in California to serve. That sum was to be all-inclusive, to pay his car payment, gas, maintenance, insurance, the whole shebang. Many of the other reps went out and bought fine new luxury cars. Not Kelly. He went and bought a used Datsun B-210, which was inexpensive to buy and very economical on gas. (Datsun is now known as Nissan for those readers who were born after the invention of electricity) The result was that he spent, on average, $200 to $300 per month, primarily on gas to cover a large territory, and pocketed the other $400 to $500 and saved that money.

Kelly and his wife Patricia bought their home in 1990 in Hot City, California. Although their income could have justified a larger more expensive home, they bought what they could afford and over the next 20 years, paid it off. The result: the couple is now in their 50's and has a home that is paid for. They could move to a more prestigious neighborhood on the golf course, but choose not to. They have peace of mind. Kelly said, "We have always lived far below our means."

When the housing bubble burst in California, Kelly and Patricia were looking for a second home on the coast to get away from the blistering summers in Hot City. They were able to find a nice place on the beach in Southern California at a good price that they will enjoy in their retirement years. The result of a lifetime of "living below our means" has resulted in two houses, paid for and peace of mind.

BOTTOM LINE

Peace of mind is boring....and wonderful!

ACTION STEPS:

- Where feasible, buy a house you can afford and then use a fixed interest loan that cannot increase in interest rate or payments.

- Pay an additional amount to shorten the length of the loan.

- Re-finance when interest rates drop, if you can qualify.

- Paying down the principal on the loan improves your loan to value ratio and increases the possibility of re-financing during periods of low interest rates.

- Generally, avoid paying "points" on a loan. Theoretically, points paid will reduce the interest rate on the loan. Always run the numbers to see how many years it takes before you reach the crossover point, that is, the point at which the "points" are offset by the lower interest rate on the loan. Points are often a glorified way to provide extra compensation to the lender. If you sell the property after a short time, or re-finance, you have paid the cost of the points without realizing the long-term gain of the lower interest rate. **"Points" are an egregious example of "Needless Enrichment".**

- Absolutely never take out a mortgage that has any sort of back-end fee or early termination charge or penalty, even if you think you will stay in the property past the expiration of the penalty period. Circumstances can change.

Home prices and values in the future

Throughout recorded financial history, housing prices have generally trended upward, but have experienced boom and bust cycles in that process. The period of the *Dead Money Decade of 2000-2009* saw a huge run-up followed by a bust. The great lesson of history is that it will repeat itself, so one can reasonably predict that there will be future boom and bust cycles in the years ahead. Here are some thoughts for evaluating a purchase going forward.

BOTTOM LINE

Remember that the "boom time" won't last forever.

In a "Boom" period.

Boom periods are characterized by over-hyped sales pitches such as "Hurry up and buy before all the houses are sold and you are left living on a park bench" or "Prices will never be this low again" Yeah, right.

Every time we go through such a period, people come up with all sorts of "creative financing" techniques to help buyers qualify for the purchase. The result is a greater number of buyers, which increases demand and pushes prices upward, perhaps artificially upward. At some point, as price increases reduce the number of qualified buyers, or if demand slackens, then prices fall and the bubble bursts.

ACTION STEPS:

- When prices are very high, buy only if you can truly afford the property using the 80/20 loan to value ratio.

- Buy in a "boom market" if you reasonably believe that you will keep the property for the foreseeable future and you like the property.

- Ask yourself, *"What if the values drop 20%?"*, *"What if I/we decide to move or get a job in a new city?"* That kind of sober evaluation can help you make a better choice.

- Be especially wary of a bubble in an area that has only a single major source of economic growth and activity, such as a city with either one major industry or one major employer. If that industry or employer moves or closes, then the entire area is impacted by the ripple effect.

When the Bubble Bursts

A sudden drop in real estate values may be a disaster, or an opportunity, or have no impact on you at all, depending upon your circumstances.

If you bought a house in a boom period and you financed it properly with a fixed interest rate loan and you (or you and your spouse or partner) maintain your employment– don't panic–keep making your payment and ride out the downturn.

If you are "upside down" (owe more than the value) and have an adjustable rate mortgage and can't re-finance, get help immediately if possible from either your lender or work with a reputable firm. (Be very careful to evaluate loan assistance companies as there are scam artists out there.) Walk away only as a last resort, but move heaven and earth to avoid this path.

Evaluate the long-term prospects for your property – the long-term economic prospects for the area. An area that has a strong employment base has a better chance of recovery than a single industry area.

A downturn may be an opportunity for you to buy a place at a better price. If you have saved and maintained your credit rating, you may be able to get a bargain. However, remember that there will always be a reason that the property is a bargain, especially if the economic circumstances of the area have changed. If you buy a bargain, be prepared to keep it.

ACTION STEPS:

- Get as "bullet proof" as possible when you buy.

- If you get "upside down", get help from reputable sources.

- If a bargain presents itself, carefully evaluate every aspect.

CHAPTER 5

INVESTMENTS

Thou Shalt Not Covet Thy Neighbor's Stockbroker

Jack Allensworth was feeling pretty good about life in 1999 with a successful construction company, a fine home in prestigious Fig Garden, a loving wife and family. He had built a solid, diversified portfolio with his broker, Harry Wieder, a former body builder and weightlifter turned stockbroker with a brilliant analytical mind who had carefully studied the markets and had a firm grasp of investing in stocks. In 1999, the portfolio had generated a total return of just over 32% (total return is the combination of dividends, interest and capital appreciation). By contrast, in 1999, the Standard & Poor's 500 Index had returned a very respectable 21%, so Jack felt very good indeed that his broker's advice had resulted in a return of over 50% better than a passive market index.

One Saturday afternoon, Jack happened to chat with his neighbor, Lyle Folsom. They discussed getting their yards ready for the winter, local politics and then the subject came around to the incredible run up in the value of high tech stocks. "Yeah" said Jack, "I've made over 32% this year." "Is that all?" replied Lyle. "My guy, Bob Sluffe at Rock Solid Resources has generated over

67% this year for me and says we are likely to double the account next year. These tech stocks can't lose!"

Instantly, Jack was incensed that his broker, Harry had made him a paltry 32% whilst his neighbor's stockbroker had returned twice as much. His opinion of Harry had turned 180 degrees in a moment.

The phone call bright and early the next Monday was short and crisp. "Why hadn't Harry made 67% like Bob Sluffe?" Jack wanted to know. Harry patiently explained that Bob had apparently bought a number of high tech stocks and that although they were doing well at the moment, there was no guarantee that they would always do so. Jack remained unconvinced and moved the account to Bob Sluffe that day.

History records the "dot com bust" of 2000-2001. Many of the high-flying tech stocks that were based upon hoped-for returns proved to be ethereal. A few years later, Jack happened to run into Harry at a chamber of commerce meeting. Jack looked a bit sheepishly at Harry. "You know, you were right. I should have listened to you instead of my neighbor and his stockbroker."

* * *

The tale was all too familiar. Jack had bought every tech stock under the sun, most at or near the historic market high. When prices began to slide, he hung on and rode to the bottom before capitulating and selling most of the positions for a huge loss.

Harry was never one to say, "I told you so", and together they put what remained of Jack's portfolio into to a more properly diversified allocation. When the meltdown of 2008 came, Jack was able to weather the storm, avoid panic and carry on.

BOTTOM LINE

There will always be returns that are "too good to be true".

ACTION STEPS:

- Research and understand assets in which you invest.

- For risky or speculative investments, use only money that you can either afford to lose, or at the very least, money that you do not anticipate needing for income for a long period of time.

- Understand your emotional gut level response to sharp downward fluctuations in market values. Only get on the roller coasters you can handle.

Safety vs. 'Greed' aka "The Sleep Factor" vs. Growth "Trading Sleep For Money"

Whether in prosperous or tough economic times, there is always a push-pull regarding safety. Many people equate safety with the idea of not losing their capital. This concern for preservation of capital is always juxtaposed with the human desire for growth. Or put in today's idiom, "Fear versus Greed."

Historically, financial advisors have been concerned with the twin issues of preservation of capital and growth of capital. The issue is profound with regard to retirees who may live for 20, 30 years or more in retirement. It is important to both preserve their capital and to have at least some hedge against inflation. If the disaster of 2008 is any lesson, then if we must choose between capital preservation and inflation hedge, we must surely focus on capital preservation. Although the concern about the impact of inflation is valid, the absolute value of the capital itself must be preserved. If we can preserve capital, then we can take some of our assets and position them for an inflation hedge. Preserve capital first, and then address inflation.

A further issue about capital preservation comes with regard to how much capital to use during one's retirement. Many retirement income planning tools will make a comparison between "Capital Preservation" versus "Capital Depletion". The capital preservation model will assume that the retiree lives off the earnings of the capital, while the capital depletion model will have the retiree spending both earnings and a part of the capital each year.

The preservation method will always show a smaller income stream than the depletion method. The two downsides of the depletion method are that as the capital is consumed, there is less capital to continue earning a return. The further problem is determining how long the retiree is going to live and most importantly, what happens if the capital "depletes" before the retiree 'expires'?

My recommendation is to use the capital preservation method to the longest extent possible. I have observed that almost all retirees prefer this method on psychological grounds. There is something very comforting about seeing a sum of money staying the same or growing slightly and conversely it is very unsettling to see the capital diminish. However, I also see cases where capital is used due to circumstances that unfold (long-term care, deadbeat children, etc).

Since the capital preservation method requires more capital to provide a desired level of income than the capital depletion method, your goal is to create a sufficient amount of capital.

How do we account for safety?

Safety for each person is going to be a function of what we know as the "sleep factor." Some clients will want 100% of all their assets invested in ways they considered totally safe or stable. Other clients will want very few assets in a stable environment because they hope to get a higher rate of return and don't lose sleep worrying about the risks involved.

Generally, most advisers recommend that the younger a person is, the more aggressive the individual can and should be as an investor, and conversely, the older a person is the more cautious one should be. However, personal temperament plays a huge role. Some younger people may be very risk-averse and want to have all funds in safe positions while older investors who understand and are comfortable with risk may still want to have a fair amount of their portfolios in more aggressive positions well past their retirement age. This may be especially true of the affluent older investor who has a safe, fixed cushion and can be more aggressive with the balance.

My preferred strategy is to provide a **base that is safe and stable, with very little fluctuation of capital, and devote some capital to growth**. The first question is: What "safe" investments are available? The second question is: How much of one's assets should comprise the "Base of Safety" and how much should be allocated to "Growth with Volatility"?

The answers to these fundamental questions depend on a combination of age, temperament, and timeframe for use of the capital or income from it whether generated by interest or dividends. Generally speaking, any money that you expect to need in the next three to five years, either for current income or for some major purchase, should be held in an account that is either stable or has very limited volatility. This ensures that you will have the funds when needed without having to liquidate a long-term position at the wrong time, incurring loss.

The safest investments are FDIC (Federal Deposit Insurance Corporation)-insured bank accounts and CDs. As long as you are under the FDIC limits, currently $250,000, your money is considered safe, backed by the U.S. Treasury.

The next level is generally considered to be fixed-interest annuity accounts issued by life insurance companies with very high ratings from the four major rating agencies. In some states there may be a state guarantee fund or pool that is available up to certain dollar limits to protect the policyholder. None of the state guarantee pools are as ironclad as the FDIC program, however, and ultimately the policyholder of an annuity is dependent upon the solvency of the insurance company that issued the annuity.

In practice, I have seen several insurance carriers become insolvent over the past 25 years, and what happens is that the state in which the insurance carrier is domiciled will typically seize the company, operate it temporarily and then sell the company, either all or in part, typically to another insurance company, so that the state only has to cover any shortfall after liquidating the failed insurance carrier in an orderly manner.

Next on the scale are **government bonds**, issued by the federal government, states, cities, and special districts such as water, power, and transportation districts. U.S. government bonds by definition are safe from default, since the US government can print money or raise income taxes to meet its obligations. That said, investors should always bear in mind that the value of a bond will fluctuate based upon rising or falling interest rates. As interest rates rise, bond prices fall, and vice versa. But if held until maturity, bonds can always be redeemed for par value, or face value, of the bond.

Municipal bonds may be revenue bonds, supported by revenue, such as electricity or water prices or bullet-train passenger fees, or general obligation bonds, those for which the city or district and ultimately its taxpayers are on the hook. They offer investors the benefit of federal tax-free income and, if the investor is a resident of the state in which the bond is issued, freedom from state income tax on bond earnings.

Municipal bonds, however, do not offer a guarantee (unless the issuer has purchased a guarantee insurance wrapper, generally available only to municipalities with AAA credit rating). Therefore, the investor is at risk if either the municipality itself fails, in the case of general obligation bonds, or, for revenue bonds, if the project doesn't earn sufficient revenue to pay back the debt. Generally speaking, the investor looking for safety in a municipal bond should buy a BBB or higher-rated bond.

Safety with Growth Strategy

A strategy that may be very appropriate for the risk-averse investor who has a relatively long timeline is what might be called the "safety with growth" strategy.

Let's assume an investor has a lump sum of money, $100,000 for our example, and wants to ensure that the value of the $100,000 never goes down. The investor wants to protect the value of that money against inflation.

Thank God I Paid Cash For The Rolls!

The investor could take the full $100,000 and put it in a single CD, or purchase several CDs with varying lengths of time and interest rates in what is known as a ladder CD arrangement. Each time interest is paid from the CD(s), the investor takes that interest and dollar-cost averages it into investments with potential for more growth, such as individual stocks.

No matter how well or poorly the stocks (or other investments) perform, the investor will always have his or her original $100,000 in the CD, so the dollars that are at risk and subject to volatility are only the earnings. The benefit of this strategy is that the investor has principal protection, especially if using an FDIC-insured CD, and has the potential for growth with the interest from the CDs invested in an investment portfolio.

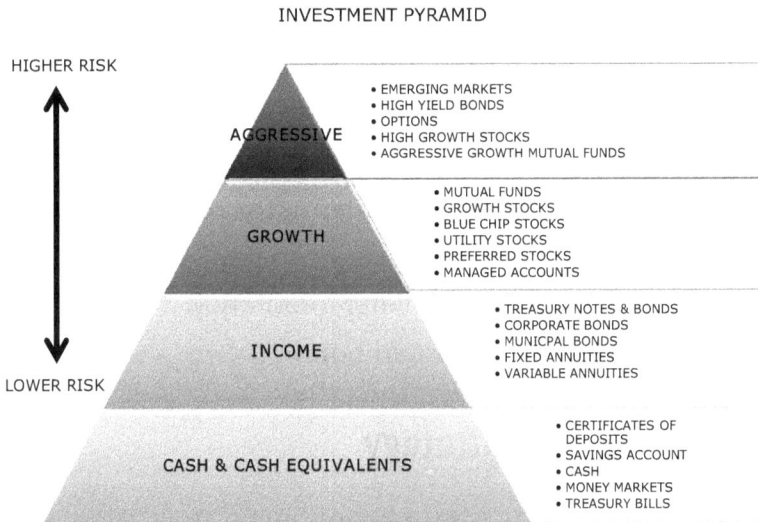

INVESTMENT PYRAMID

HIGHER RISK

AGGRESSIVE
- EMERGING MARKETS
- HIGH YIELD BONDS
- OPTIONS
- HIGH GROWTH STOCKS
- AGGRESSIVE GROWTH MUTUAL FUNDS

GROWTH
- MUTUAL FUNDS
- GROWTH STOCKS
- BLUE CHIP STOCKS
- UTILITY STOCKS
- PREFERRED STOCKS
- MANAGED ACCOUNTS

INCOME
- TREASURY NOTES & BONDS
- CORPORATE BONDS
- MUNICPAL BONDS
- FIXED ANNUITIES
- VARIABLE ANNUITIES

LOWER RISK

CASH & CASH EQUIVALENTS
- CERTIFICATES OF DEPOSITS
- SAVINGS ACCOUNT
- CASH
- MONEY MARKETS
- TREASURY BILLS

Investments Overview

Successful investing first requires a general understanding of the kinds of investments and their unique characteristics, their strengths and weaknesses and the manner in which their values fluctuate based upon market circumstances and the economic outlook.

- Stocks (also known as Equities)

- Bonds

- Real Estate

- Annuities

- Commodities

- Collectables

- Business Interest

- Notes

Let's elaborate on each of them...

Stocks

Stocks are a method of owning a fractional interest in a company. When a business is incorporated, it issues shares of stocks. These shares can then be sold on one of the stock exchanges if it is a publicly traded company (unless it is restricted stock). If the firm is privately held, there may be little or no ready market for the shares. For a firm that is listed on a national or region stock exchange, the shares may be traded as long as there is a buyer and seller.

Stock prices are supposed to be a function of the present value of the estimated future earnings. That is, in theory, the price of the stock, or at least the range of its price, should be ascertainable. The reality is that not only is the price of the stock based upon "facts", but also upon emotion. So a stock with good fundamentals make suffer in price due to market fears and conversely, a stock with suspect fundamentals may do very well if the market is swept up on positive emotion. The "dot-com" bust of the early 21st century was a classic example of companies with very high stock prices based upon speculation without sound underlying economic fundamentals.

US Stocks are sub-divided into three classes based upon their capital size. Large Capital stocks are 5 billion and above, Mid Capital stocks are 1 to 5 billion and Small Capital stocks are those under one billion in size.

Stocks are often classified as either a "growth" stock or "value" stock. Growth stocks are those that have higher price/earnings ratios. They are stocks that are deemed to have good future prospects.

Value stocks are those stocks whose industry is out of favor, or the specific company is struggling. The idea of the value stock is that it can be purchased at a comparative lower cost than a growth stock.

It's the day after Thanksgiving or the day after Christmas and eager buyers are lining up in front of retail stores, often in the wee hours of the morning in freezing cold weather for the chance to buy some TV, computer, the latest video game or other "must-have" widget at what is perceived to be a substantial savings. The discount may be 40, 50, 60% or more off the normal retail price. At these savings, there are often more buyers than "widgets" and a buying frenzy ensues.

Yet during periods of great volatility in the stock market, if a quality blue chip stock is suddenly selling for 40, 50 or 60% off its historic price, there are no buyers to be found. The reason for this is the great paradox of the market. Although investors are always advised to buy low and sell high, many investors do exactly the opposite.

When stock prices have dropped and you are considering investing, either adding to a position you already own or buying a new stock, you must evaluate whether the stock is low in value due to fundamental problems with that company, whether the industry is out of favor, a general pessimistic economic outlook, or some combination of these factors.

During periods of hysteria and panic, when stock prices move on emotion rather than on fundamentals, you must carefully research the underlying fundamentals of a company whose stock you are considering purchasing and determine how strong that company is within its own industry and how that industry is faring in comparison with the overall economy.

Bonds

Bonds are issued by corporations, the US government, states, municipalities and districts. A bond is simply a loan to the entity involved. You the investor are a creditor; you do not have an equity stake.

The bond is issued for a set term, e.g. 10 years. At the end of the term, the bond issuer pays the bond holder the "par value". Some bonds will allow the issuer the option of redeeming the bond prior to the end of the term. This is known as a "callable bond". Usually, the issuer has to pay the bondholder a premium to "call" the bond, meaning to redeem the bond prior to its original maturity.

The essential concept that investors need to understand about bonds is that the market value will fluctuate daily based upon increases or decreases in interest rates. Bond prices move inversely with interest rates; as interest rates go up, bond prices go down and as interest rates go down, bond prices go up. An example will illustrate the point.

You buy a 10 year XYZ Corporate bond for $1,000 at 6% interest. The bond will pay you $60 per year (usually $30 semi-annually) for 10 years and then the bond will mature at par value ($1,000) 10 years from the date of issue.

If interest rates two years from now for a new bond issued by the same company is at 7% (assuming the company has the same credit rating), then if you sell your 6% interest bond, you will get less for your bond since an investor can earn $70 versus $60. Conversely, if interest rates are at 5%, your bond will be more valuable since it pays $60 versus $50. You now have a premium bond. Keep in mind that if you pay a premium for a bond, the issuer will still only pay the par value when the bond matures.

Since investors will often be faced with two seemingly contradictory investment objectives, one being the desire to lock in an interest rate for a long period and the second objective of not being locked in for a long period of time if interest rates go up, many investors will use a ladder bond strategy. The ladder bond strategy means that an investor will buy some bonds with short, intermediate and long-term holding periods, for example a one year, a five-year, and a 10 year bond. That locks in a long-term interest rate on the 10 year bond while still giving the flexibility on the short-term bonds. If interest rates are higher when the short-term bonds mature, those funds can be reinvested at a higher interest rate. Conversely, if interest rates have dropped, at least the longer-term bonds still carry on at their original higher interest rate.

Real Estate

> *Real estate has long been favored by investors because, unlike a stock, you can touch and feel it and drive by and see it.*

Real estate is one of the most popular forms of investing. Real estate has long been favored by investors because, unlike a stock, you can touch and feel it and drive by and see it. Real estate may take the form of a single family house, duplex, apartment complex, office building, shopping center, raw land, farm land or warehouse and industrial property.

Since real estate can be purchased for a down payment and a loan (rather than only all cash) there is both the advantage and disadvantage of using leverage (borrowing). If the property appreciates by a greater percentage than the interest rate on the loan, then the investor has used leverage to his or her advantage. If on the other hand the value of the property declines, then leverage magnifies the loss.

Let us focus on investment real estate.

The simplest example is a **fixer-upper house**. The house is offered at a discount because its condition is less than ideal. The question, of course, is whether the "fixer-upper" label is an issue of cosmetics, paint, carpet, etc., or because of major structural problems, such as roof or foundation replacement. Determining value depends upon what needs to be done, what the costs will be to repair the problems, and what the market might be like after the repairs are made, depending on how long they take.

The second issue, using the house as an illustration, will depend upon the market conditions of the particular neighborhood, city and region in which the house is situated. In some instances, no matter how many repairs you make to the property, there is a finite upper level of value that a house can achieve simply because of where it is located. (The old maxim, "Location, Location, Location")

The final issue about buying in a down market is the investor's own ability to hold onto the asset until it appreciates. This requires both a practical financing mechanism to make it possible and that comfort level or sleep factor that we've described to be able to hang on if the asset loses value during the holding period.

From a financial perspective, the ability to hold onto the asset will depend on whether the investor can buy it outright or whether he or she will have to borrow or margin in order to be able to acquire the investment. If any sort of borrowing is involved, then the investor has to be reasonably comfortable that he or she can meet the debt service not only during, but beyond the anticipated holding period. If the holding period turns out to be much longer than originally estimated, the investor must be able to meet the cash flow obligation, even if he or she suffers a reversal in some other area of their finances.

Annuities

Annuities are an insurance product that is designed to provide a stream of income either now or at some point in the future. In their modern configuration, they are available as fixed interest, variable or indexed annuities. I do not recommend using an indexed annuity as will be discussed below.

Annuities may be an "Immediate Annuity", meaning that the income stream begins right at the start of the annuity or it may be a "Deferred Annuity", meaning that you put money into the contract and it grows for years, even decades before you begin to take an income.

Fixed or guaranteed interest annuities are just what they appear to be. The rate of interest is set by the issuer, usually for a certain number of years (1 year, 3 years or 5 years). At the end of the guaranteed period, the interest rate will renew at prevailing rates. Most contracts will have some minimum guaranteed interest rate. The minimum used to be 3%, now we often see 2% as the floor.

Indexed annuities are the "bad boy" of annuities. They will often have a guaranteed interest rate (for example 5%) for the annuitant and then have the potential for a higher rate of return based upon some formula such as 70% of the Standard & Poor's 500 stock index. That means if the S&P index goes up by 10%, you get 70% of that gain or 7% for that year. The trade-off is that you do no worse than 5%. However, there are trade-offs that are unseen. One is that frequently index annuities have very long surrender charge periods or they are so-called "two tiered" annuities where the surrender charge never goes away and the only way to get the higher account balance is to annuitize the plan. The further issue with the index annuities is that since they are technically a "fixed interest" product, the representative does not have to be securities licensed, even though the return is based on some equity index. If a plan is going to be based in part upon an equity index or bond index, then the person selling it should have either the FINRA Series 6 or Series 7 licenses. It is splitting hairs to not have this license. Finally, index annuities may be subject to a "market value adjustment" at surrender. Most "market value adjustments" use a Byzantine formula that not even a rocket scientist could understand. There are very few instances in the financial planning world where we give an absolute or use the word never, but this is one of those times. **Never buy an indexed annuity! Period**.

Many financial commentators will observe that there are fees associated with annuities. You do pay a mortality and expense charge. You do pay if you buy any of the living benefit riders. All these fees will mean that the internal cost of an annuity will generally be higher than using equities or bonds with a similar investment objective. Whether to use the annuity depends upon whether the value of the tax deferral and the guaranteed death benefit are useful and needed by the investor. There is no "every situation" answer here, so here are the guidelines to make an evaluation.

Use a fixed interest annuity if you require a guaranteed rate of interest and stability of principle and income tax deferral.

Commodities

Commodities are raw materials. They include, gas, oil and coal and foodstuffs like soybean, pork bellies and corn. They may also be precious metals, gold, silver, copper, industrial diamonds. They are frequently traded on the futures market. Trading in commodities requires specialized knowledge, a big bank account, and intestinal fortitude. Even the savviest investors have the occasional involuntary "wallet emptying" ceremony where their dollars go to "money heaven".

For the investor who wants to have some participation in commodities, consider a stock in a company in a commodity industry. This gives you exposure to a particular commodity, but with (hopefully) an expert who understands both the commodity and the external factors that impact the price. Always do your own research, and understand how seemingly unrelated events can impact your investment before investing.

The key with any commodity investment is that they can fluctuate wildly in value, based upon market supply and demand, political instability, war and civil unrest, the global economic situation and in the case of foodstuffs, weather. Seemingly unrelated events can converge to drive prices up or down quickly. Volatility is the watchword for commodities.

Collectables

Collectables are a convergence of money and emotion. A collectable is generally an item whose value exceeds its underlying intrinsic worth. The value over the intrinsic value is the factor of rarity, demand by collectors, unique historical provenance and sentimental or emotional factors. An old car, previously owned by a famous person, may command a higher price than a similar model of the same make because of the link to the celebrity, yet both are the same in terms of appearance and driving performance and will cost the same to repair and maintain.

Collectables often have a generational aspect. People will often collect things that are evocative of their youth. Grown men will often decades later buy the "dream car" they could not afford during their high school or college days. Understand that future generations may not have the same evocative attachment and thus the price of a collectable may fall in the future. The key with collectables is to buy things that you like and enjoy owning. Be extremely cautious of anyone selling any collectable as a "great investment". If it is such a "great investment", then why are they selling? Of course, many people have and do make money buying and selling collectables. If you choose to do so, become thoroughly knowledgeable, do your research, and network with reliable experts and collectors in the field.

Thank God I Paid Cash For The Rolls!

Collectables are always subject to market swings: in boom times, prices will go up, especially if there is "stupid money" chasing them. In downturns, collectables will suffer as there are often more sellers and fewer buyers. A downturn, of course, can be a great opportunity for a collector to buy something long desired at a lower price.

Business Interests

Business can take many forms and so the market value will vary. The key for most business owners, especially sole proprietorships and small partnerships is to have a realistic idea whether the business could be sold and if so for what price. Many small business owners will look to the value of their business as the bulk of their retirement. I have often heard business owners say "The business is my retirement plan", meaning that they did not perceive the need to have an IRA or other pension plan.

That approach is valid so long as the business does hold value (especially if the person or persons who own it are no longer involved) and if there is a willing buyer at an appropriate price. I recommend that a business owner consider the following steps:

- Even if a sale is decades away, think in terms of building a business that can operate without you.

- Build value that is tangible to a buyer.

- Implement an IRA or qualified pension plan for both the income tax deferral and just in case some "hiccup" occurs and the business value diminishes. Having other savings helps diversify your total portfolio.

- Find your successor owner and work out a phase-in period. Too many business owners make an abrupt change which can cost customers and money.

Some businesses, especially those that are professional services, may not readily lend themselves to sale or may have a fairly low value.

Notes

Notes or "paper" are often associated with real estate, but may be secured by other assets, or be unsecured. A note may be created when you sell a property and take back paper to help the buyer make the purchase. The note may be one that has been created by a private party or by a firm. Depending upon the circumstances, the note may be offered at a discount from its original value. Since every note is unique, be sure to thoroughly research any purchase of a note. You must understand the value or the underlying asset and forces that can impact its value.

Should I buy in a down market?

The short answer to the question of whether to buy in a down-market is one's ability to determine the value of an investment and specifically to determine if an investment opportunity is significantly undervalued and then have a clear understanding of what events need to occur for that value to increase.

The second consideration is how long the investor anticipates it will take for the proposed investment to recover and show a gain. Money used to invest during a down market should be funds that the investor does not anticipate needing for at least the period of time it will take for the investment to show a good return. Additionally, the investor should assume that it will take longer than anticipated for the hoped-for return and plan accordingly.

"Do You Still Have the Fillings In Your Teeth?" - Identifying and Avoiding Unscrupulous People and Companies

As a consequence of being a "car guy" with a bug not only for Rolls-Royces, but also that much rarer, but equally eccentric obsession known as being a "Chrysler Man", in the mid 1990's, I was looking at buying a nice mid 1960's Imperial to be a proper companion to my 1956 Chrysler 300B.

There was an advertisement in one of the national "want ad" auto journals by a private seller, Lloyd Lugnut, who had a large number of such cars and parts, located about three hours from my home. One fine Saturday, I drove out to his place, a vast bone yard of 1950's and 1960's Detroit iron baking in the hot California sun. Many of the cars were beyond restoration and were "parts cars". Lloyd did have a beautiful 1965 Crown Imperial for sale. On the test drive, the transmission smoked and then seized. We hobbled back to the bone yard and needless to say, I didn't buy the car!

A few days later, by chance, I happened to speak on the telephone with Erik Evergood, a member of both the Chrysler 300 Club and Rolls-Royce Owners Club, who has an extensive collection of cars. I off handedly remarked that I had been out to see Lloyd Lugnut. "Do you still have the fillings in your teeth?" Erik exclaimed. He then went on to explain that poor old Lloyd had a very bad reputation for dishonest dealing throughout the car collecting community. I had dodged a bullet thanks to a timely "Failure to Proceed" on the part of the normally reliable Torqueflight transmission. It seems that bad things happened to good cars under Lloyd's "care".

There is an old adage that says "You can't make a good deal with a bad person". In what may or may not be correctly referred to as "the good old days", people more often did business with people and businesses in their own locale, whom they knew personally. That did not prevent shady or dishonest dealing, but it did give one a chance to make an intuitive, subjective evaluation of the person or firm before conducting business. Further, there was more societal pressure on a local business to conduct business honestly, as "word of mouth" could spread quickly within a community if a business owner were dishonest.

In today's world where more and more transactions are done via the internet with people and firms in every conceivable corner of the globe, it becomes harder to make that sort of face to face evaluation. Yes, many industries are subject to both internal and external regulations, compliance and audits, but the old Latin phrase "caveat emptor" (buyer beware) is more applicable now than ever. The financial scandals of the early part of the 21st century occurred even with regulations in place. Some industries have no self regulatory mechanism or external oversight of any sort in place and the customer is truly at the mercy of the ethics of the people running the firm.

Always do your research, not only regarding the features and benefits of a product or a service you are considering, but also the reputation of the person or firm. If anything seems incongruent, investigate and ask questions. Get independent, third party information and ask for references and then call those references. None of these steps can always prevent doing business with unethical people or companies, but it can minimize the chance. If you find that a seller is "less than honest", get competent help to resolve the issue as soon as you become aware of the problem.

"There Was a Lake There!" - Identifying the Warning Signs

"There was a lake there, I swear to God there was a lake there" - Actor Burt Reynolds' character in the movie "The End", defending a shady real estate subdivision development which had the word "Lake" in the name of the community (but possibly not an actual lake in the development). Here is a real example of identifying a potentially "shady" proposal.

The caller on the other end of the line seemed like a pleasant young fellow. He introduced himself and began to describe the limited partnership he was offering for sale. He didn't know that I was in the securities business, so I mentioned that I had the NASD Series 6, 7 and 22. Without missing a beat, he replied "Those are good investments also."

The big warning signed flashed! Why? The salesman did not know that NASD Series 6, 7 and 22 referred to securities licenses, not investments. The fact that he did not recognize the term "NASD" (National Association of Securities Dealers, now known FINRA, the Financial Industry Regulatory Authority) meant that he was not licensed to sell securities. He was in fact selling an unregistered security, giving the impression that he was a stockbroker, yet he was not licensed. It further meant that the real estate limited partnership he was offering had not been subject to any due diligence by any firm or analyst. Now, it is possible that the offering could have been legitimate, there might have been a real property, there might have really been a "lake" there as the above quote remonstrates.

But the reality is that the potential for the offering to be shaky at best and an outright fraud at worst was very high. The best case scenario for that offering was that its organizers would make more

106

money than the investors. I politely demurred to buy the investment.

Let me say at this point that even an investment offered through a reputable brokerage firm that has been reviewed by a firm's due diligence analysts does not ever guarantee the success of the investment, nor does it make the investment suitable for every investor. Not every investment is appropriate for every investor. For example, an investor who is risk adverse should not make a speculative investment. An investor who requires the funds in the next six months should not put those funds in an investment that is not liquid for the next five years.

Life lesson learned

"Bulls make money, Bears make money, Pigs get slaughtered."

The above quote refers to the old adage in the stock market that the smart investor can make money but that the greedy investor most surely at some point will lose money. This is the story of three real estate agents but it could be three people in any sales or marketing or selling situation:

When I was selling my house on the socially wrong side of the tracks in bad old Cold City, California, I decided to list it and sell it myself. As a financial planner with 30 years of selling experience and having done some real estate transactions in the past I was comfortable with the myriad of details and rather looking forward to the excitement of selling. I listed the house and wisely stated "Broker Participation Invited" in all the advertisements so that a buyer's agent could earn a commission of 2% if he or she would bring a buyer.

The day after I listed the house within one hour of each other I received two telephone calls at polar opposite ends of the spectrum.

The first call was from a bright young real estate agent Blake who indicated that he had a prospect, a young newlywed couple who lived only two blocks away from the house I was selling. They were interested in looking at the house and Blake asked if it would be possible for them to view the house that evening at 7 PM. Although the house wasn't absolutely quite ready since this was a Thursday and I was preparing for a weekend opening, I knew that it was better for the prospect to see the house than to tell them no and risk having them buy another property.

Whilst I was cleaning the house and getting it ready for the 7 PM Thursday appointment a second broker called. He had seen my listing and knew that the house was being sold by its owner. I could tell from his questions that he was looking for a way to disturb me about my ability and chances to sell the house on my own so that he might have an opportunity to get the listing. He asked questions such as 'how did I arrive at the selling price' and 'what will I do if I don't sell the house' and 'how long do I think it might take to sell the house'. Without letting him know that I was onto his game I answered his questions in an upbeat positive manner showed no sign of weakness or doubt and expressed to him that I was rather looking forward to the fun of selling the property. Finally we got to the question of the commission and he asked how I arrived at the 2%. I indicated that was the standard amount. He immediately became quite upset and told me in no uncertain terms that the standard was 2.5% to even 3%. The conversation ended shortly thereafter.

Which agent might one suppose will be more successful? The first agent, who saw a new listing, called a client, called the owner and arranged for a showing all on the same day, or the realtor who called an owner with no buyer in sight and attempted to sow the seeds of doubt? Even if I had failed to sell the house on my own I most certainly would not have picked the second broker to list the house, so in either event that second broker wasn't going to make any commission no matter what the percentage.

(The "rest of the story" is that I did in fact sell the house two months later. Whilst I was meeting with the new owner, he mentioned that his agent had showed him many houses, but "She didn't show me this one!" His agent missed out on what would have been over $15,000 in commission because she was far too "above it all" to show a lowly "for sale by owner, broker participation invited" pile of lumber on the wrong side of the tracks in Cold City! Of course, in Cold City, $15,000 is chump change.)

* * *

This example pertains to a real estate transaction, but it could be any situation in life. The first agent, Blake looked at an opportunity and saw it as just that, an opportunity and took immediate action. If he does that a hundred times in the future, he will sell some houses and earn some commissions. The second agent looked at the same set of facts and saw only the negatives and decried that the margins weren't high "enough", that his income wouldn't be "enough". He was looking strictly at the marginal difference of a deal he wasn't going to get in the first place. If he calls a hundred owners and whines and berates them, he will sell exactly zero houses and earn exactly nothing! The third agent walked past the opportunity altogether, even though she had a well qualified buyer.

How many times in our own lives do we look at situations where we bemoan and decry what we are not going to get, what we can't have, what isn't possible instead of looking at what in fact we can do in a constructive manner, what opportunity we might be able to achieve, what goal or accomplishment is feasible, what is possible? That is not to suggest that particularly in an unfair situation we should "take it lying down", but it does mean that if the circumstances and times are hard, **we must always look for the opportunity rather than dwell on the negatives.**

CHAPTER 6

RETIREMENT PLANNING

Retirement Planning Checklists:

- Set goals and priorities.

- Set your [current, or retirement?] budget, showing fixed and variable expenses.

- Set a minimum dollar amount or percentage of every paycheck to go into retirement savings.

- Increase savings percentage or dollar amount as income increases.

- Understand and maximize your employers' retirement plans.

- If self-employed, implement a retirement plan for yourself.

- Study and understand investment options; get professional advice as needed.

- Use debt and credit cards wisely, with the goal of eliminating all debt before retirement.

- Monitor and make changes as needed.

- Determine and list all assets and sources of income: Social Security and pension income, personal savings and investments.

- Determine if you can, will or want to work full-time or part-time in the same industry or in a second or third career.

- Discuss plans and coordinate with your spouse.

- Rebalance investments based on age-appropriate income needs and "sleep factor" – park them where you won't be up nights worrying about your financial security.

- Review and implement appropriate health insurance plans including Medicare, Medi-gap (Medicare supplemental insurance), and possibly long-term care (e.g. nursing home) insurance.

- Enjoy life!

Retirement Accounts

There are three major categories of retirement accounts:

- Employer-provided plans

- Individual retirement accounts

- Self-employed retirement plans

We will look at all three types of plans. In some cases, an individual may have two or more of these plans, depending upon their employment situation and history. After we explore how all of the different plans work, we will look at several ways in which the plans may be integrated and coordinated, both during the accumulation phase and during retirement, the payout phase.

Retirement accounts can help you achieve your long-term savings goals. In addition to that basic function, they also have several powerful effects on income tax that should be fully understood and evaluated so as to reap the maximum income tax benefits. (As always, we advise the reader to consult with his or her accountant or other tax professional before starting any retirement plan.) Let's explore these in detail...

Employer-Sponsored Retirement Plans

Employer-sponsored retirement plans will generally fall into one of two major categories. The first is known as the defined benefit pension plan. The second category is known as the defined contribution plan. We will explore both in detail.

Defined Benefit Plans

The defined benefit pension plan is a qualified plan in which the participant is guaranteed or promised a specific dollar benefit, usually a monthly income benefit. The benefit is generally calculated on a formula based upon the employee's income and his or her number of years of employment. A typical formula might look like this; the employee receives a monthly benefit equal to 40% of his salary if he worked for the firm for at least 20 years and 50% of his salary after 25 years of service.

Defined benefit pension plans were very common in private industry following World War II and are still frequently seen in union and government pension plans. They have become less common in private industry for nonunion employees since the

1980's. They have fallen out of favor with employers because they require companies to fund the plan each year, regardless of how well or poorly the company performed. The plan must provide the promised benefits no matter how well or poorly the investments in the pension trust supporting the benefits are performing.

The funding issue for the company can be problematic in both good and bad times. In a poor year, the firm may find that it does not have the cash flow or need the income tax deduction for the required contribution. Conversely, in a good year, if the investments in the pension plan have appreciated, the required contribution may actually be smaller and so the company cannot put in a larger contribution even though it could meet the contribution and could use the income tax deduction.

The rules and requirement to fund a defined benefit plan each year have sharply curtailed the attractiveness and number of such plans.

The key advantage of the defined benefit plan for employees, on the flip side, was a reliable, certain dollar amount that could be depended on at a specific age to provide retirement income. Such plans were and are a real benefit to the employees who work either most or their entire career for one company.

The disadvantage of these plans occurred for employees who changed jobs every few years and were never vested in much or any benefit.

These plans were part of the more paternalistic approach that was common in corporate America in the post-World War II era. The idea was that you worked for one company for your entire career and the company took care of you. That model seldom exists today, and it is the main reason why individuals must be more diligent than ever in planning their own financial future and stability.

You Must Become Your Own Defined Benefit Plan Manager

With the decline of the defined benefit model, each one of us must think and act like a defined pension plan manger with the exception that instead of managing a sum of capital for many employees, **you are managing the funds for yourself and your loved ones**. Just as a pension manager, you must accumulate the money during your working years and then manage the payout for you and for your spouse or partner.

Distribution issues about defined benefit plans

Those who do have a defined benefit plan will be asked to make a very significant decision, either at retirement or shortly before retirement. That decision is whether to take the full monthly benefit, sometimes known as the unmodified benefit, or Option A, (depending upon the terminology in the plan), or to take a reduced amount of benefit during your lifetime so as to provide for a continued benefit for your spouse should you die first. (This is called the survivor benefit.)

For example, you could take $3000 a month, unmodified, or take a smaller "modified" amount, perhaps $2500 monthly. Upon your death, your surviving spouse would continue to get one-half, two-thirds, or perhaps even the full "modified" amount ($2500 in our example), depending on the plan details.

Occasionally there will be the odd plan where there is no cost for the survivor benefit, or where the cost for the survivor benefit is very minimal. Always have the defined benefit pension plan administrator or the human resources department of your company, union, or employer give you a complete breakdown of all the options, ramifications and timeframe in which you must make the election as to which benefit distribution plan to select.

When you take a smaller "modified" benefit in order to provide for your spouse, what you have done in essence is to purchase a life insurance policy, even though there is no actual policy and it is not labeled as such. The modified survivor pension benefit is most advantageous for couples in cases where the pensioner lives only a short time after retirement and the surviving spouse lives for years or decades after the pensioner's death. The unmodified full pension benefit is best when the participant lives for a long time in retirement and the spouse survives only by a short period of time or not at all.

Each defined benefit plan and each individual's situation is unique; carefully evaluate each benefit option and have a qualified accountant or financial planner review your options.

Defined Contribution

Defined contribution plans have become very popular since the 1980s, and most frequently appear as 401(k) plans. These plans gained favor with employers because the employer's share of the contribution was generally based upon either a percentage of payroll or a percentage of the employee's contribution. This gives the employer a much more easily ascertainable dollar amount and far greater predictability as to the funding levels required from year to year.

Furthermore, in most plans the employer has the option and ability to reduce or eliminate its funding contribution, giving the employer a safety valve during bad economic times.

It's not so rosy on the worker side, however. The downside of the defined contribution model is that **the employee has no guarantee of a total dollar amount or a specific monthly income amount that will be available upon retirement**. If either the employee or the employer does not contribute enough, or if the investment returns are poor, then the employee will find him or herself retired without adequate capital to enjoy retirement. The fact that there is no guarantee of either a total dollar amount nor a specific monthly income makes it imperative for the employee to understand, fund and monitor his or her plan. As stated above, you must be your own pension plan manager!

Since the defined contribution model, and in particular the employee-funded model such as a 401(k), is now the most common type of plan it, is vital for employees to understand and manage their plans to get the maximum value out of them.

The first thing for an employee to do is:

- Get a copy of the employer's plan.

- Get all of the pertinent material and also the website address of either the plan administrator or the plan's investment house.

- Read and understand the material that is provided, especially with regard to how the employer match or bonus or profit-sharing mechanism works.

In many plans, for you as the employee to get an employer contribution you must make a contribution yourself. It is vital to understand the formula and then always strive to contribute at least enough to maximize the employer's contribution. The employer match should be regarded as additional income, even though it is deferred.

If the formula or the information provided is confusing or overly complicated, ask for help from either a plan representative or from an outside source such as your CPA or financial planner.

Individual Retirement Plans

Self-funded individual retirement plans fall under one of three categories:

- Traditional Individual Retirement Account (IRA)

- Roth IRA

- Rollover IRA

* * *

Individual Retirement Account (IRA) and Roth IRA

The individual retirement account (IRA) is available to anyone with earned income. The amount contributed may be deductible based upon one's adjusted gross income and whether one is covered by an employer-provided pension plan.

Roth IRAs were developed as a result of the pension act of 1996. The concept is 180° different from the traditional IRA. With the Roth IRA, the participant does not get a current income tax deduction – that is, for the year in which the contribution is made. The trade-off is that distributions from the Roth IRA are not taxed when taken, normally during retirement, if taken properly under the rules.

A qualified financial planner or CPA can work through a hypothetical model comparing the net present value of the Roth IRA to the traditional IRA. The bottom line is that the Roth IRA is most effective for participants who anticipate that they will be in the same or higher income tax bracket when the distributions are taken during retirement, compared to when the contributions were made during their working years. Conversely, if our account holder expects to be in a lower bracket in the future, then he or she may well be better off taking the current income tax deduction on the traditional IRA and taking out the money later in a lower tax bracket.

For example, a young person just starting out in his or her career who expects to be successful and build a good portfolio, and who also may inherit a large estate at some point, may very well want to use the Roth IRA in the early years, in their 20s and 30s, while their marginal tax bracket is low, assuming that when they reach their retirement years, their marginal tax bracket will be much higher.

The benefit here is that they may forgo a 15% marginal tax bracket deduction when the funds are contributed, but enjoy tax-free income when their marginal tax bracket is 30% or greater.

The opposite may be true for many people, such as those making a relatively large income today, but with fairly small portfolios and little or no expected inheritance. These folks may very well be better off taking income tax deductions today, while in a 30% or more marginal tax bracket, anticipating that they will be in a 15% tax bracket during retirement. In such cases, it makes far more sense to get the deduction at a 30% level and then withdraw the funds, paying taxcs on them at a 15% rate during retirement.

What you are evaluating here is which plan is the most 'tax efficient" based upon your current tax bracket and what is a reasonable expectation of your tax bracket during retirement. This calculation of course, requires a bit of "crystal ball" work. No one can predict what tax rates will be 10, 20 or 30 years from now and no one can guarantee what their assets and income will be in the ensuing decades. So all of us have to make a reasonably educated estimate of what will happen in the future and plan accordingly.

The examples above demonstrate how the suitability of the Roth IRA versus the traditional IRA will vary from one person to another and why we cannot give a blanket statement as to the suitability in all cases. As always, crunch the numbers with your accountant and/or financial planner. Ultimately, there is no right or wrong in having money in either kind of account. Either one beats having no retirement account.

Consider both, especially if you are "semi-retired."

One side benefit of accumulating funds in a Roth IRA as well as in taxable retirement accounts and income-producing portfolios is especially applicable to what we will call the semi-retired person.

This might be someone in their 60s or 70s who has retired from the primary career but continues to work either on a part-time basis or perhaps on a serial basis – for example, they do some consulting work for three months and then they don't work the rest of the year. Another example might be someone who takes an interim position for a one- or two-year period.

This is the perfect time to utilize a Roth IRA. If the person has a comparatively large level of earned income in one year, she may opt to augment that income with distributions from the tax-free Roth IRA, since the distributions from the Roth IRA won't add additional tax. Conversely, in years of little or no earned income during retirement, the participant will be better off taking monies out of a taxable account, at least up to the amount that the person begins to approach the 25% marginal tax bracket.

Using this method, the participant minimizes or defers the income tax, making the Roth IRA a very valuable retirement planning tool.

Rollover IRAs

The Rollover IRA is an IRA that is used when you get a distribution from an employer's plan and do not want to take money out immediately. The Rollover IRA lets you accumulate the money until age 70 ½. You can begin taking money out without a tax penalty after age 59 ½. You must follow the correct rollover procedure so that your funds are transferred from the employer's plan to your rollover account directly.

The Rollover IRA can be invested in a wide variety of investment options. You can begin taking income after age 59 ½ and must start taking distributions after age 70 ½.

In some cases, you may be able to roll money from a prior employer's plan into a new employer's plan. Check with your new company to see if their plan allows for rollover money.

Other Roth IRA retirement planning techniques

- Wealth Transfer Strategy

- Market Volatility Strategy

- Tax Harvesting Strategy

* * *

Wealth Transfer Strategy

One of the great benefits of the Roth IRA is that there is no required minimum distribution. That means the holder of the Roth IRA never has to take income from the account and can therefore pass the entire account on to heirs. This is a useful technique for a wealthy person who doesn't need to take the distributions to meet income needs.

Market Volatility Strategy

If a client has determined that he or she would like to convert some or all of a taxable traditional IRA to a Roth IRA, he or she should consider taking advantage of market turndowns to make that conversion.

Example: Suppose a person has $100,000 in a fully taxable IRA account. The market takes a drop and the account is now worth $70,000. If the person converts the account to a Roth IRA, he or she will pay tax on only $70,000, rather than on $100,000. The account holder must be able to qualify under the applicable rules for making the Roth conversion based on his or her adjusted gross income for the year the conversion is done. Additionally, as with all Roth conversions, the account holder should pay the tax with "clean money," meaning with funds from outside the Roth account itself. Using the account's own dollars, known as "dirty money," defeats the purpose of doing the Roth conversion as the fund is now smaller and therefore the future value will be proportionally smaller than if the taxes are paid with outside funds or "clean money".

Once again, the reader is advised to consult with a qualified tax professional before making a Roth conversion.

Tax harvesting strategy

The tax harvesting strategy is another one of those situational moments that has the potential to be **very beneficial under the right set of circumstances**.

Suppose that you worked for a large corporation for many years and have left that firm to start your own business. You had $250,000 from your former employer's 401(k) plan that you put into a rollover IRA. If during the first year or two your new business has a net operating loss, you may find it possible to convert some or all of the Rollover IRA – enough to offset your loss – to a Roth. The upshot here is that any amount of the conversion that merely gets you back to zero dollars of income for the year means that you have effectively converted those dollars of the taxable rollover IRA at no tax cost. If you still have a loss to carry forward, you may be able to continue to offset your losses over the ensuing years and continue to convert part or all of the taxable traditional rollover IRA to the Roth. This technique, of course, requires careful advance planning, but if used properly, it provides a tremendous opportunity to pay little or no tax on dollars that otherwise would have been taxed and to permanently put them into an account where you will never pay tax on them if withdrawn properly. *Always have your CPA run the numbers and make sure all the ramifications are examined before using this strategy.*

How your pension plan can save your bacon

In the Beginning....Why?

The wonderful comedian, Red Buttons, was a frequent guest on celebrity roasts. He would look into the audience and with a pained expression on his face and asked, "Why are we giving this famous celebrity a dinner?" And so it is with many people who get a 401(k) enrollment form shoved at them; they ask "Why"? Why should I get in the plan?

The answer is three fold: income tax savings today, retirement income tomorrow, and ultimately, the goal of reaching financial independence. The goal is to achieve financial freedom. It may not mean stopping working, but it means that at some point in our lives, we can get to the place where we don't have to work to meet at least our basic necessities.

Most people initially focus on the income tax savings and in the short run that is a significant benefit. However, the real benefit of the plan is the value that the semi-compulsory savings via the automatic payroll deduction provides. Thus, over time, the account builds. The employee has both the tangible benefit of the dollars in the account, but also the intangible benefit of the peace of mind that being financially secure can bring.

How much is enough?

Many financial planners and advisers talk about achieving financial independence. Each individual will define financial independence differently based on their own circumstances. A good way to evaluate it is to divide financial independence into two categories, Tier 1 "needs" and Tier 2 "wants".

The first category will be one's basic needs, and the second category will be what we might call the "wants" or the luxuries. Of course, different people will have a different definition of what is a need. We all need shelter, but that might be anything from a rented studio apartment to a large four bedroom home in the suburbs or even a mansion on the hill. As you begin your 401(k), determine the amount of money and the amount of capital that you will need to achieve at least what I call Tier 1 that provides what you consider to be the basic necessities of life.

After determining the basics, then it's important to determine those Tier 2 things that would be nice to have that would come under the heading of wants or luxuries. These items will vary from person to person. For some it might be travel by going very economically. Others will pay for first-class airplane tickets and the best suite in every hotel.

The key to financial independence is for all of us to get to the point where we do not have to work for wages or run our own business in order to meet a standard of living that we find both acceptable and desirable. This does not preclude the idea that we might still continue to work for the fun of it or to afford the "extras". But for all of us, we are going to get to the point where we simply can't or don't want to work for income, and therefore we need the capital to be able to generate an income stream.

> *The key to financial independence is for all of us to get to the point where we do not have to work for wages.*

Some people may find that their income and capital is large enough to provide the basic Tier 1 necessities, and then continue working to provide for Tier 2 luxuries or wants.

Getting Started

The single most important part of the 401(k) plan is just getting started with the first dollar. The systematic contributions are the basis of everything else that follows. Even if you think you can't afford it, just start making contributions. Even with a small amount of money, a small percentage saved begins to help you develop the habit of systematic savings; you'll thank yourself over the years.

Determine the amount you can save. The traditional guideline for saving has always been 10% of income. The concept is that saving 10% of pay per year would mean that after 10 years, one would have saved a whole year's income, plus have the earnings. **For example, a person earning $50,000 per year who saves $5,000 per year will have $73,917 at 7% interest in 10 years.**

Although a 10% savings rate is the "textbook" rate, the savings rate for each person will vary based upon circumstances. For the person for whom the 10% rate is a very high hurdle, then we will have to start at a lower rate.

The most important aspect is to start saving, even at 1% of income, rather than not save at all. Although a lower saving rate may not be adequate from a long-term standpoint, the greatest need is to get started, even with a few dollars and begin to build. The first dollar a person contributes to a plan earns the most interest over time. Over time, the amount saved can and should be increased to build to the level that will achieve the desired result.

A good time to add to the percentage of contribution is anytime you get a raise or any time you pay off a bill such as a credit card. If you immediately save some or the entire raise into the 401(k) or save some or all of the former credit card or loan payment into the 401(k), the easier it is to get the money into the plan before some other item consumes it.

The other aspect of the 10% guideline is that it is by no means a maximum savings rate. Those that are able, or can discipline themselves to do so, should try and exceed that level to 15% or more. In practice, we often see people who are approaching retirement save a substantial part of income. Sometimes this is used to "catch up" from years where the savings rate was low.

The Japanese have historically had a national average savings rate of 15%. That is part of the reason that Japan has been economically successful. That high savings rate has meant that the nation has a vast amount of capital for investment. It also creates an economically successful and financially stable population which is beneficial from both a social and economic standpoint. The United States, by contrast, has a personal savings rate at around 5%, which, from a national standpoint, is not adequate. Since that is an average, it means that while some are saving a good amount of earnings, many Americans are saving nothing, or worse, "dissaving", meaning spending more than earning. The first point is, start at a level that you can afford, with a bit of a stretch, and then build the amount over time.

Understand and maximize any employer contribution

Many 401(k) plans offer some sort of employer contribution in either the form of a match or profit-sharing contribution. In some cases the contribution will be readily determinable as in the case of a match. In other cases, the amounts may not be ascertainable, such as a yearly profit-sharing based upon the firm's results. In all cases the employee should be familiar with the formulas for qualifying for the employer contribution.

If there is a set match, then the employee should try and maximize the formula. For example, the plan might state that the employee gets a 100% (dollar for dollar) match on the first 3% of salary contributed and then 50% on the next 2% of salary contributed. For our employee earning $50,000 per year, the match would work as follows:

Thank God I Paid Cash For The Rolls!

3% of pay is $1,500 (Company match 100% = $1,500)

2% of pay is $1,000 (Company match   50% = $500)

If the employee defers 5% of pay, that is $2,500 per year. The employee also gets the company match of $2,000. So the employee's balance is $4,500 before earnings. If the employee has a traditional deductible 401(k) and is in a combined 30% state and federal income tax bracket, then the employee saves the income tax on the $2,500 ($2,500 x 30% = $750). Thus, the employee has saved $750 in income taxes so the net after-tax cost of the deferral is $1,750 ($2,500 - $750 = $1,750)

The employee has an after-tax cost of $1,750 and yet has $4,500 (before earnings) in the plan at the end of the year. If the employee had contributed a total of 10% of pay ($5,000), then the numbers would be as follows. The company match would be the same, $2,000, since the formula only matches on the first 5% of contributions. The employee would have the $5,000 of his/her deferral and $2,000 of employer money for a total of $7,000 prior to earnings.

The tax result in a 30% bracket would be a savings of $1,500 ($5,000 x 30% = $1,500). So the after tax cost of the deferral is $3,500. The employee has an after tax cost of $3,500 and $7,000 in the plan prior to earnings. Under this scenario, the employee has effectively doubled their money in the first year.

Investment Options

The choice of investment options at the outset of starting a 401(k) is less important than getting the money in the plan. Initially, simply getting into the plan and funding the plan at an adequate level is the single most important element.   However, as time goes on, and the account grows, the investment choices become more and more important as the size of the account gets larger and larger.

Most employers' plans today will offer a wide choice of investments. A typical plan will offer 10, 20, 30 funds or more. Some employers may also offer a brokerage window which will allow the participants the opportunity to buy individual securities or separate accounts or mutual funds not available under the basic choice.

- The first step for the employee is to get all the information the employer furnishes about the individual investment choices.

- The second step is to determine your time horizon.

- The third step is to determine one's risk tolerance. This will be a combination of both time before retirement, one's prior experience with investments, and a third more subjective factor that we call the "sleep factor".

Generally, the longer one has until retirement, the more investment risk one can assume, because there is a longer period of time for markets to rebound. Also in the early stages of one's 401(k), if the markets are down or low, the dollars that are contributed go in and purchase more shares or units of the investment options and therefore you are buying at a lower price. The concept here is that if the markets rise over time, the value of your shares or separate account units will rise and you will have achieved a growth in your fund.

Conversely, the less time one has prior to retirement, in general, the less risk one should take. However, given that the 401(k) account in most cases will be paid out over the person's retirement years, which may be 20, 25 years even 30 years or more, the employee should still keep at least part of the funds invested in a way that can help to provide a hedge against inflation. For example, if the average inflation rate is 3% during one's retirement, it means that on average prices will double in a 20 year. A person retiring at age 65 may find that by the time he or she is 85 prices have effectively doubled. Therefore, it is important that your funds be structured in a way that will help you to maintain some inflation hedge.

Many plan sponsors today offer a risk tolerance questionnaire or other planning device that asks both hard fact questions such as how many years do you have before retirement, what is your age, and also merging in "soft facts" questions such as, "if your investment went down by 20% would you sell it, hang on, or buy more of it?" Every participant should use one of these risk tolerance questionnaires and models both at the outset of getting into the 401(k) and periodically take the quiz again based on one's updated circumstances to determine if the investment models that have been selected still meet the person's goals and objectives.

The Default Investment Account

If an employee does not make an investment selection, then the plan sponsor has to put the funds in the default investment account. Historically this has been either a money market account or in some cases, a fixed interest account, if such an option was available under the plan. After the new pension law changes, the default option now in most plans will be what is sometimes known as a time-based or mix of equities, bonds and cash. The concept here is that potentially a balanced or asset allocation fund may provide a greater long-term rate of return than a simple money market. I always recommend, however, that employees make their own investment choices rather than not making a selection and having the default option. Instead, it is important for each participant to take an active role in managing one's own monies.

> *No matter where you are today, you will be better off*
> *tomorrow if you save a regular amount each paycheck.*

For some employees later in their working years, the value of the 401(k) plan may well exceed the equity in their home or even exceed the total value of their home. So in essence the 401(k) account balance for a 40 or 50 or 60-year-old employee may at some point be that person's single greatest asset. For this reason, it is imperative for each employee to take a hands-on approach to managing this valuable capital.

"I am ready to retire – Now What?"

There are many factors to consider when deciding when and how to take money out of the 401(k). The basic rules are that you must begin taking some distributions by the time you are 70 ½ years old. Prior to that age, there are several options.

The first is to determine if you are planning on working at all during retirement. If you are going to work part time or work at a second career, then you may not require income from the plan. You spouse might be still be working or you might have other assets that can provide income. If you are completely retired and require income, then here are your options. You can use a rollover IRA. You can then take one of any number of income options shown below.

REQUIRED MINIMUM DISTRIBUTION

REQUIRED MINIMUM DISTRIBUTIONS (RMDs) GENERALLY ARE MINIMUM ACCOUNTS THAT A
RETIREMENT PLAN ACCOUNT OWNER MUST WITHDRAW ANNUALLY STARTING WITH THE
YEAR THAT HE OR SHE REACHES 70 ½ YEAR OF AGE OR, IF LATER, THE YEAR IN WHICH HE
OR SHE RETIRES.

RMD FORMULA: THE AMOUNT IN IRA ACCOUNT / THE DISTRIBUTION FACTOR =

AGE	DISTRIBUTION PERIOD	AGE	DISTRIBUTION PERIOD
70	27.4	93	9.6
73	24.7	95	8.6
75	22.9	97	7.6
77	21.2	100	6.3
80	18.7	103	5.2
83	16.3	105	4.5
85	14.8	107	3.9
87	13.4	110	3.1
90	11.4	113	2.4
		115 and over	1.9

If you have at least $5,000, you can keep the money in the employer's 401(k) plan and take income options that are provided under the plan.

If you are moving on to another company, you may be able to rollover your account to the new employer's 401(k).

Income Options

"72t" Rule – Under this odd sounding title (named for the IRS code section), you keep your account balance and take a systematic amount based upon your attained age. Prior to age 59 ½, this rule can be used to take money out without paying the 10% early withdrawal penalty. However, if you elect to take money prior to age 59 ½, you must take a level amount for the greater of five years or until you reach age 59 ½.

For example, a 52 year old would have to take income until age 59 ½ and a 57 year old would have to take a level income until age 62 to meet the five year requirement. Between ages 59 ½ and 70 ½, there is no minimum or maximum rule as to how much income to take. One takes as much or as little as need or in some cases, no distributions and you can vary that amount from year to year. You pay income tax based upon your tax bracket. For people in their 60's who then also do some work, they may want to take less in years where they earn more and take more in years with less income to get the best tax efficiency. A qualified CPA should be used to make the tax evaluations.

Beyond age 70 ½, you have to take at least a minimum amount based upon the 72t rule. At age 71, for example, this works out to 3.56% of the account balance. Therefore, if you had $100,000 on December 31, 2010, you would have to take at least $3,560.00 in 2011 to meet the minimum requirement. You could take a larger percentage if needed. Each year as you grow older, the minimum percentage increases based upon your attained age.

The benefit of the 72t rule is that it can preserve some of the capital for your use during your lifetime, and any balance can be passed on to heirs. The disadvantage is that you must manage the account in a manner that will preserve the capital and provide income for your lifetime. Poor investment choices or taking too much too quickly can deplete the fund.

Traditional Pension Option – most plans will let participants take a guaranteed lifetime income (with a spousal survivor benefit if appropriate). The benefit of a lifetime income is that one has a guaranteed lifetime benefit that one cannot outlive. The disadvantage is that the capital balance is converted into the income stream so there is no account balance to draw upon. Further, the benefit to heirs will generally be only the surviving spousal benefit if selected, or the balance of a number of years certain such as 10 or 20. Under years certain, if you elect a lifetime income with a 10 year certain period and then you live 7 years, your heirs will receive 3 more years of payments. If you live 12 years, then the heirs do not receive any benefit.

Fixed Number of Years – Under this option, you (or your heirs) get income for a set number of years, from 5 to 30 years (usually in 5 year increments). You get the income for the number of years selected. If you pass on before all the years of income have been paid, your heirs receive the balance of the unpaid years of income.

So Which Option is Best?

The best choice will depend upon your income needs, your ability and interest to actively manage the account (if using the 72t rule) and how important or unimportant it is to have access to the principal. If the goal is to have a set amount of income, then a life income option or a long fixed period account may be appropriate. If the goal is to actively manage the funds and have control of the account balance, then the 72t rule approach may be best.

Other factors to consider will be whether you and or your spouse continue to work and if you have other sources of income, such as an investment portfolio, real estate or the sale of a business. The key as we have said all along is to begin to fund the plan.

Pensions and 401(k) s are tremendous tools in financial planning. They are often misunderstood, but a little education and understanding of what you can and what you can't do with these financial instruments can provide a huge benefit both today while you are in the earning and accumulation stage and tomorrow when you are in the enjoyment stage.

With 2008's stock market meltdown, many 401(k) plans became what was half-jokingly known as a 201(k). Despite the market downturn and resulting loss of worth in these funds, understanding and utilizing the 401(k) plan and coordinating it with Social Security income and an employer's defined benefit plan can be invaluable.

The key during retirement is to structure one's income so that there is a combination of a fixed-dollar income stream, such as Social Security or a defined benefit pension plan on one hand, and a capital account such as a 401(k), IRA, and/or profit-sharing plan that has the potential for growth to offset inflation.

Broadly speaking, there are two major risks that employees face in retirement. One is the risk of running out of money – that is, one takes too much, too quickly out of an IRA or 401(k) plan and depletes the account with many years of life still ahead of them.

The other risk is that inflation may erode the purchasing power of one's retirement income. This is especially true for the early retiree, for example, age 60 or 62, and enjoys an above-average life expectancy and lives into their 80s, 90s or even to age 100 and beyond, which is becoming more common every day. This retiree will require income for potentially 30, 35, or even 40 years. Even at a 3% inflation rate, every 20 years the purchasing power of every dollar will effectively be cut in half. The retiree who retires at age 62 with a $5,000-a-month income stream will find that at a 3% inflation rate, that amount will have the purchasing power equivalent of only $2,500 at age 82, and only $1,250 age 102.

So the challenge is to provide an income that you cannot out-live and, in a perfect world, which has some reasonable inflation protection, especially for those retirees who live to an advanced age.

We do this by evaluating first the sources of fixed income which may be Social Security and potentially a defined benefit retirement plan. This might be a government or union plan or occasionally may have been offered by a private employer. A couple will want to check and see if one or both of the spouses are covered by such a plan.

Next, we want to evaluate what accumulation accounts we have, such as an IRA, profit-sharing, or 401(k) plan, any kind of defined contribution plan where the retiree owns and controls the account balance. With these types of clients we have flexibility as to how much to withdraw until the client reaches age 70 ½. We know what the account balances are and we can estimate what the income might be each year.

The next areas to consider for retirement planning are all the non-retirement plan assets that an individual or couple might have. These would include investment real estate, investment portfolio, collectibles, life-insurance cash values, annuities and possibly the sale of a business or professional practice. All these items should be items that can be quantified to some reasonable degree of certainty as to the value at the beginning of retirement.

In some situations it may be appropriate to plan or anticipate an expected inheritance; however, care should be taken in planning one's own retirement that any future inheritance takes into account the circumstances of the person who will be giving the bequest.

Even if there is a potentially fairly large inheritance, the current holder of that asset may need to use a substantial portion of those funds during his or her lifetime for their own lifestyle or for long-term care, final expenses and estate taxes. Additionally, depending upon the makeup of the expected inherited item, the asset value may rise or fall. **All those variables should be accounted for in making a plan for an inheritance. Generally speaking, one should err on the conservative side in terms of estimating when that amount might actually be seen.**

Now that we have determined what the base level income is and what our investment assets are, we can back into how much of an income stream we are going to need during retirement. One method is to do a pro forma budget and determine how much income one needs for both basic expenses and how much one needs to add what we'll call the "goodies" such as travel, indulging the grandchildren, buying that fancy new car, your second home. Determine a number that is the minimum required and a higher, nice to have or desirable number.

Take the ideal income per year, subtract out the guaranteed income stream amount, and the remainder amount is the amount that you need the accumulation funds to provide for a stream of income. A quick shorthand method is to divide that required number by 5% and that will tell us how much capital we need to have in order to generate that much income.

Let us use a 5% income withdrawal rate as an example for some-one with a total of $1,000,000 in income producing assets, excluding the primary residence and items such as collectibles that do not generate income. With $1,000,000 at a 5% interest assumption we can generate $50,000 per year of income as long as the fund earns 5% or more. Then we won't be spending the principal amount. In a perfect world you want to generate a return greater that the percentage you take out as an income stream.

Some financial analysts will recommend using an even more conservative assumption of as low as 3% or 4% income stream from our capital. The lower the interest assumption the more likely that your capital will be preserved and the longer it potentially will last: the younger and the better one's health is at the outset of retirement, the more one should consider using a lower interest assumption.

The flip side is that for a later retiree or someone who has retired and worked part time well into their 70s, that individual may be more comfortable using a higher interest assumption.

The key in any case regardless of the interest assumption used is to monitor that withdrawal rate frequently and make adjustments especially downward if the withdrawal rate becomes too aggressive.

Income Stream

The question that comes up for retirees with most or all of their retirement (apart from Social Security) coming from their capital accumulation account becomes a matter of how to provide an income stream, even through a prolonged down market. The strategy is as follows: historically financial advisors have recommended that clients have at least three years' worth of the income stream in a fixed or very safe investment account. Returning to our million-dollar example; if we're going to withdraw $50,000 a year of income per year, one would want to have at least $150,000 of that million in a savings account, CDs, or other fixed assets. Essentially one should have three years worth of the income stream in a fixed position

Given the recent market fluctuations of 2008 we might want to expand that from three years of income to four or even five years of income so that in our $1,000,000, one might have $200,000 to $250,000 in a fixed position. Then if the markets remained down for a substantial period of time one would not have to withdraw from an equity position or a real estate position during a down market.

The strategy here is that during periods of good times during up markets for examples (say mid-2007) we would then harvest gains meaning, that we would take off the table some of the gains we have earned and put that in cash or CD's against the advent of a downturn.

Depending upon one's investment tolerance, some retirees will have a far greater percentage than what we have just shown in a fixed or relatively stable investment account, but the amount shown above should be considered the minimum guideline to give the greatest potential for a reliable stream of income without having to liquidate an equity position in a down market.

The key with this strategy is that it requires periodic monitoring by the retiree and his or her advisors, and it requires the discipline to take some chips off the table during up markets. It is human nature when the market is going up to say "let it ride" with the idea of it's going up it will continue in the upward direction. It may feel counterintuitive to harvest some gains in an up market, but if done on an appropriate basis it will provide the protection during down markets.

A key issue here may also be the nature of the capital accumulation accounts that are involved. All things being equal, it will be more tax efficient to move funds within a retirement plan than it may be to move assets that are not in a retirement plan. A retiree's retirement plan may own shares of XYZ Corp. and the retiree might also own shares of the same corporation in a general brokerage portfolio outside the retirement plan. Selling the XYZ shares that are held in a retirement account will have no immediate tax impact until the values are withdrawn from retirement account, whereas selling the same XYZ shares in the brokerage portfolio account will incur a capital gains tax.

It will always be important for the retiree to understand the tax implications of decisions made both in and out of qualified retirement plans.

Borrowing from your 401(k)

Borrowing from your 401(k) is a **double-edged sword**. Used properly – in the right circumstances for the right reason – it can be a useful tool. There are a couple of concerns to be aware of, though, to avoid having the 401(k) loan become detrimental to your financial health.

The 401(k) loan was developed as a means of letting people use funds during their working years, primarily for things such as home down payments, college education for children and unforeseen medical expenses. The benefit of borrowing from one's 401(k) is that you do not pay the 10% early withdrawal penalty for withdrawing funds from the account before age 59½, nor pay regular federal and state income tax that you would owe if you took an early withdrawal.

The 401(k) allows you to borrow up to 50% of your vested account balance, up to $50,000. You must re-pay the loan over a 2 to 5 year period by payroll deduction. All the interest paid on the loan goes into your account.

The biggest pitfall to be aware of with the 401(k) loan is the fact that if you separate from your employer – whether you leave by choice or by lay-off or a non-voluntary reason – you must repay the full balance of your 401(k) loan within 60 days. So if you don't plan to stay with your employer for the anticipated lifetime of the loan – generally two to five years – or if you suspect your employer may run into tough times and be forced to lay you off, then the 401(k) loan is unadvisable (unless, of course, you have a source of funds or another credit line to make a lump-sum payment to pay off the loan).

Another cautionary note about the 401(k) loan is the tax treatment of the interest participants pay on the loan repayment. Even though all of the interest paid on the 401(k) loan goes back to the employee's own account, that interest is not tax-deductible when it is paid on the loan – that is, when it goes into the account – yet when it is withdrawn at retirement, you pay tax on it, just like all the other money in the account. The loan repayment interest gets the worst tax treatment possible, with in essence a non-deductible contribution but a taxable withdrawal. The technical term for this is "tax-inefficient."

However, although the 401(k) loan interest is tax-inefficient, the result needs to be compared with borrowing the same amount of money via either a credit card or a home equity line of credit, for example. Leaving aside the interest rate difference for now, the bottom line is that with any other source of credit, the interest you pay will never come back to you. With the 401(k) loan, your interest payments go back into your retirement fund, even though you do have to pay tax on it when you take distributions at retirement.

Also, the tax-inefficiency of the interest payments can be mitigated by borrowing as much as possible from your Roth 401(k) if you have one. The benefit of the Roth 401(k) is that, while as with the traditional 401(k), the interest paid on loans is not tax-deductible, under Roth treatment, this interest (now part of your total Roth 410(k) funds) will not be taxed when withdrawn during retirement, i.e., it is not tax-inefficient as with the traditional IRA. So ideally, if we need to borrow from our retirement funds, we want to borrow first from the Roth portion and then from the traditional (taxable) portion.

Generally speaking, the 401(k) loan should only be used strategically for major long-term needs – specifically to help with a home purchase or tuition and other education expenses.

The 401(k) loan should be used very sparingly and very carefully as a debt consolidation device. Although it's very tempting to pay off all of your high-interest credit cards with a 401(k) loan, unfortunately it is also very easy for many well-intended people to set up a 401(k) loan, consolidate their credit card debt and then turn right around and start running up their credit cards again. Soon, they're back with high credit card debt AND a 401(k) loan to pay off!

The 401(k) loan can be useful to consolidate debt if you truly have made a commitment to cut down on new spending and if your credit card interest rates are exorbitantly high. If you can go from paying 15% or 20% interest to a credit card company to paying 5% or 7% on a 401(k) loan – AND you are disciplined enough to not rack up that credit card debt again – then it is a good strategy. Even though the 401(k) loan is "tax inefficient," as discussed above, at least you are getting the interest payments instead of your credit card company, and the total amount of interest you'll pay will be far less.

For whatever reason you take out a 401(k) loan, my final piece of advice is to pay it off faster than the scheduled repayment, if you're able to. Other than the stretch-out for new home purchases, 401(k) loans terms are two to five years. In practice, I've seen most people take the five-year amortization schedule. Most 401(k) plans let participants pay extra principal on the loan. This doesn't reduce the regular payment, but it does shorten the number of years until the loan is paid off – and reduces your overall interest payments.

In addition to reducing your overall interest payment, because the 401(k) plan offers guaranteed borrowing power, it is important to pay it off so that those funds are always available in reserve. It further minimizes the risk of having an unpaid 401(k) balance if you leave your employer.

Advanced Techniques – Deferred Compensation

Deferred Compensation plans are a unique and creative way for a company to recruit, retain and reward key executives. The following summary will focus on the design concepts and the financing techniques. A sample illustrating the accounting for these plans is included in a separate attachment. Although all these are areas are inter-related, it is useful to examine each component separately.

Design Concept

Deferred Compensation is an open book and you are writing the chapters. The company determines the plan design and the participants.

Deferred Compensation plans typically allow selected employees the opportunity to defer a part of their income. In theory, this could be 100% of an employee's income, although many plans have a limit such as 30% or 50% of income. There can be different limits depending upon the type of compensation. The plan might have a limit of 25% of base salary and then allow for a 100% deferral of any bonus. The deferral percentages might have a graded scale, either up or down. For example, an employee could be allowed to defer 20% of pay on the first $250,000 of compensation and 50% on amounts over $250,000.

These plans can be particularly useful to highly compensated employees (HCE) executives who are covered under a non safe harbor 401(k) plan and are limited as to their 401(k) contributions. The employee can (and should) continue to contribute the maximum allowed into the 401(k) and then contribute the additional desired amount into the deferred compensation plan.

Plan participants should continue with the company's 401(k) plan since 401(k) plan assets are held in a separate pension trust and are not subject to the claims of the company's creditors. Additionally, the executive continues to receive any matching contribution offered in the 401(k). The plan can be funded entirely with employee contributions, funded entirely with company contributions, or can be funded by a combination of both employee and employer dollars.

The employer contribution can be either a percentage of salary or fixed dollar amount or a performance based incentive plan. You can have different formulas for each employee, although it usually makes sense to treat similar employees in a similar fashion.

The employer can use the plan to replace some or all of the compensation or benefit package that a talented executive might lose by leaving his/her current employer and joining the new firm. Generally, the executives who may be offered the plan are those people that are classified as Highly Compensated Employees (HCE).

The deferred compensation agreement is a contract between the executive and the employer. The employee is an unsecured, general creditor of the company. In the event of insolvency, secured creditors claims are senior, even if the company has set aside specific assets to meet the deferred compensation obligation. Because there is what the IRS deems a 'substantial risk of forfeiture" the executive is permitted to defer part of his/her compensation and not pay current income tax.

Receiving Benefit Distributions

Normally, the plan provides that benefits be paid at some triggering event, usually retirement, death, disability or termination of employment. Prior to 2004, some plans offered a pre-arranged in-service distribution. The IRS took the viewpoint that such in-service distributions could be used to manipulate income from year to year to minimize one's marginal income tax bracket. Recent regulations have effectively ended in-service distributions. The plan should be both viewed and operated as a long-term retirement program.

The plan can give the executive a choice as to how to receive benefits, either as a lump sum or over a set number of years, such as 3, 5 or 10 years or more. Because plan values are an asset of the company, conventional practice is for participants to take their distributions over a relatively short period. However, since the plan is "non-qualified" values cannot be rolled over into an IRA.

For the participant who has both a deferred compensation plan and a qualified pension plan, one strategy might be to liquidate all of the deferred compensation values first and then begin withdrawing the qualified plan. For example, an executive who retires at age 62 might take an eight year distribution from the deferred compensation plan, letting the 401(k) plan accumulate and then upon exhausting the deferred compensation plan at age 70, begin withdrawals from the 401(k) (which are required by age 70 ½). Deferred compensation plans do not have a minimum or maximum age requirement for distributions as do qualified plans.

The plan will have to state how earnings are determined. The plan can offer a fixed rate which may be tied to some published index or bond. Or, the plan can be designed to resemble a modern 401(k) plan with a variety of investment options. (These are sometimes referred to as 401(k) look-a-like plans or 401(k) mirror plans). In a plan that offers a choice of investment options, the participant is normally credited with the net investment results of the funds selected.

Financing Techniques

For the purposes of the IRS, most deferred compensation plans are structured as "unfunded", meaning that the employee does not have a claim on a specific asset. Even though the firm has set aside the employee's deferrals into a specific investment, the company, not the employee, owns that asset. Most plans (approximately 96%) do set aside money even though they are technically "unfunded". If the employee has any legal right of ownership on the underlying assets, then the employee will lose the current income tax deduction.

The money deferred by participants can go into working capital, be invested in an investment portfolio including individual stocks and bonds or placed into either Corporate Owned Life Insurance (COLI) or, where applicable, Bank Owned Life Insurance (BOLI)

The truly unfunded plan is used in about 4% of all plans. In this case, employee deferrals remain as part of the working capital of the company and are not put into a separate investment. Normally this kind of plan uses a stated interest crediting rate for the deferrals. If the company can earn a greater return than the percentage promised to the employees, then the company can enjoy the spread. However, if the company's return is lower than the amount credited to the employee, then it must cover the difference. This method can place more risk on the plan participants, since the benefit payouts will be the responsibility of future management.

Recommendations for Starting the Plan:

- Determine who will be included

- Determine deferral percentage limits

- Determine cash flow impact to the company and set an aggregate limit if necessary.

- Determine if there will be any employer contributions

- Determine method of crediting earnings

- Determine financing method(s)

I recommend keeping the design fairly simple at the outset. For example have the same percentage deferral for everyone. You can add a company match at a later date if it is not appropriate now. If an aggregate limit is required today, it can be raised as circumstances permit.

Integrating Qualified and Non-Qualified Pension Plans

Question: "How does a company go about integrating the qualified plans and the non-qualified plans?"

Answer: A company has to begin with the objective in mind. Generally speaking, the company will look first to maximize the benefits that may be available under a qualified pension plan. The qualified plan is used by many companies as a method of recruiting and retaining good employees, company contributions are tax-deductible in the year that they are made so that part of the cost of providing the pension benefit is offset by the income tax savings.

Many companies today may look to first use a 401(k) type program, which is heavily funded by employee dollars and then matched either under a safe harbor or discretionary profit sharing arrangement by the employer. Additionally, some companies may wish to use a cross-tested or age-weighted or new comparability plan, which in the right set of circumstances can focus more of the company contribution on older and more highly compensated employees. Whether any of these more advanced techniques will work will depend upon the census of the company in question, and ultimately, the amount of money that is available for the company to direct to the pension plan.

Additionally, some companies may want to layer on a defined benefit plan or bifurcate the plan, and therefore be able to offer both the 401(k) type program as well as a defined benefit plan. This type of planning will tend to benefit older employees who often are the more highly compensated employees. Several types of combination plans using defined-benefit and 401(k) may be adopted, based upon the objectives of the employer, the makeup of the employees and the dollars involved.

The amount of income that such plans will provide highly compensated employees as a percentage of that employee's salary may be inadequate for the highly paid executives to maintain the same standard of living in retirement as he or she enjoyed during the working years. Some companies may find that even with the advanced techniques surrounding the new comparability and defined-benefit pension techniques as noted above, the total tab for such plans may either be cost prohibitive or may require covering employees other than those to whom the employer wishes to provide an extra benefit. The result will be that employers will often look to non-qualified plans to provide additional benefits.

A very popular non-qualified plan is the so-called 401(k) look-alike or 401(k) mirror plan. In this plan, the executive first contributes the maximum amount allowable based upon age into the qualified 401(k) plan. The executive then has the option of deferring an amount potentially up to 100% of pay into the non-qualified plan. Money set aside under this arrangement is not taxable until the executive takes the funds out at retirement. The company may choose to match some of the executive deferrals as they do under the 401(k) plan. But there is no requirement that the company provides the match. Conversely, the company may decide to put a greater percentage or dollar amount of matching contributions into the non-qualified plan than it does under its qualified plan. The match can also be structured as a performance-based or incentive contribution.

Another very popular method of deferred compensation is the **employer funded account**, which now after the 409A regulations is the non-account balance plan. This plan type looks like a traditional defined benefit pension plan. The executive will typically get a fixed dollar amount for a set number of years upon retirement, for example, $100,000 a year for 15 years. There is no account balance per se but rather the executive has the promise of this stream of income beginning at a certain age or certain triggering event. Under these arrangements generally the entire funding comes from the employer. The employer can either use the cash flow of the business to meet the obligation, corporate owned life insurance, or taxable securities such as stocks or bonds to meet the obligation.

CHAPTER 7

INSURANCE

Insurance is an issue that most people would prefer not to think about. The reality is that you get the opportunity to pay a premium for something you don't want in case something you don't want to happen to you happens. That said, **a well-rounded insurance program is an integral part of creating financial independence**.

> *A well-rounded insurance program is an integral part of creating financial independence.*

We will examine in detail the following types of insurance and see how they fit into the planning puzzle:

- Life insurance

- Disability insurance

- Long-Term care insurance

- Medical insurance

- Property casualty insurance

- Liability insurance

Life Insurance

There is probably no other form of insurance that is as misunderstood and maligned as life insurance. When used properly, it is an invaluable tool that does something that no other financial tool can do. The event that causes the need creates the money. The problems surrounding life-insurance can generally be traced to two areas: poor sales practices and exaggerated assumptions and lapse-based pricing from some life insurance companies.

We will look at the important uses of life insurance and also point out the pitfalls to avoid.

There are five primary uses for life insurance:

- Income replacement

- Debt liquidation

- Business use (deferred compensation, loan repayment and key person)

- Estate tax and estate equalization

- Charitable Bequests

For personal life insurance the most common usage is for the first two items of income replacement and debt liquidation. When a wage earner dies, his or her salary or business income ends and the life insurance can replace some of that lost income. Additionally, the life insurance proceeds may be used to pay down or payoff a mortgage on a home or other debt.

Life insurance is frequently used for business purposes. It may be used for key person coverage to indemnify a business for the loss of a key owner or executive. It is frequently used for salary continuation and deferred compensation plans wherein the business guarantees income to the employee either at retirement or death. Business life insurance is also used where a business has borrowed from a bank and the lender wants a guarantee of getting paid back if the business owner or a key executive dies.

A fourth use for life insurance comes under the heading of estate planning. Life insurance is frequently used as a method of paying any applicable state or federal estate tax with discounted dollars and may also be used to equalize or balance an estate with multiple beneficiaries.

For example, if an estate holder has a business worth $1,500,000 and a total estate of $2 million with two beneficiaries perhaps two children, and wants to leave the estate equally divided, but also wants just one child to inherit the business, then life insurance can be used to provide extra cash to the child who is not going to continue in the business and still provide each beneficiary a fair and equal share of the estate.

"A Policy in Action"

I had a client in the early 1980's with an estate of about $2,000,000, who said to me "If I have ten dollars left when I die, I want my son to get five dollars and my daughter to get five dollars". He meant that he wanted each of his two children to get an exactly equal share of his estate upon his death. His first wife, Giselle, a lovely lady who had worked side by side in the family business, had sadly died and he later remarried happily. He purchased a life insurance policy to help pay the estate taxes. Again, sadly his second wife predeceased him some years later.

He was a smoker (as was his first wife), so the premiums were higher than they would have been for a non-smoker and he bought as much life insurance as he could afford. When he died, the life insurance still wasn't enough to pay all the estate tax, but at least we had put a dent in the bill. Both his son and daughter received an equal share of their parent's estate and the client's business is still being operated by his son to this day! Should he have bought more life insurance? Yes! Did he buy what he could afford? Yes! Should he have quit smoking? Yes! Should his first wife have quit smoking? Yes!

As we have said several times in this book, we don't always get perfection, but at least we do the right thing most of the time.

"Charity Begins At Home"

Life insurance can be an excellent tool to provide for a charitable bequest. Suppose a person regularly gives $1,000 per year to a favorite charity be it a church or synagogue, a hospital, a school, a soup kitchen or any foundation that works to serve the common good. When that donor dies, unless some sort of bequest is made, the $1,000 annual donation dies with him or her.

Suppose our benefactor takes out a $25,000 face value life insurance policy with the charity as the beneficiary. Upon the donor's death, using a 4% interest assumption, the charity will now continue to get $1,000 a year in interest from the capital of $25,000. If properly managed, this will provide the charity with $1,000 per year in perpetuity. With even better management, if the charity can earn on average a return greater than 4% but only take a 4% income stream, then over time the original $25,000 will grow in value and thus the income taken each year will rise as well to help offset the effects of inflation.

Properly structured, the donation of a life insurance policy can turn a fairly small annual donor into a comparatively large benefactor.

154

A wealthy investor may use a substantial life insurance policy and possibly along with other assets to fund a private foundation that can provide charitable bequests in perpetuity. There are a number of rules and considerations: consult a qualified CPA and estate attorney for such a foundation.

Term versus Cash Value

There have been endless debates over the merits of term life insurance versus any of the cash value forms of life insurance such as whole life, Universal life, or variable life.

I will repeat here the advice given to me in 1981 by the man who brought me into the financial services industry, Lon Tanner. Lon was the agency manager of The Bankers Life and a prince of a guy, who sort of looks like the actor Dick Van Dyke, and is a warm and generous person. He said to me, "Eric, the best life insurance policy is the one that is in-force the day you die".

What Lon meant was that it was not as important whether the policy was term or cash value but rather that **a policy was in place at the time it was needed**.

One of the absolutes that often gets trotted out with regard to life insurance is the idea that you won't need life insurance after age 65 or when you're retired or some other specified point. The idea here is that at some point you have accumulated enough assets and have little or no debt and therefore do not require life insurance to meet any shortfall. As we often point out in financial planning, there are very few absolutes and this is one example where there is not an absolute. It may be true that some individuals will reach a point where they have no debt: they have adequate income and capital to provide for themselves and their heirs, have an estate that is small enough to avoid any applicable estate taxes, and have no particular charitable bequest to make. Such a person may have little or no need for life insurance.

It is equally true that people do reach age 65 or their retirement years and still have a need for life insurance. For example, one might have a mortgage on a house or may have a significant amount of assets that are not easily converted into cash, or have a special needs child, or one spouse has a larger pension than the other spouse, or one spouse is significantly older than the other spouse and is concerned about income to the surviving spouse and that pension ends upon that spouse's death or a client may wish to provide a favorite charity with a substantial bequest. In all these cases life insurance may very well be an appropriate financial method to achieve the desired result. As we often say with most things financial, there is no "one-size-fits-all".

My own opinion is that you should determine the reasonable amount of insurance that, along with your other assets, will provide the desired result and buy that amount of coverage. Then determine the amount of premium that fits your budget and "back into" how much is term and how much is cash value.

Determine the level of income continuation, debt reduction and where appropriate estate liquidity and charitable bequests required. These goals will help you determine the face amount of the policies needed and the amount of premium that you can reasonably afford; then determine the type of policy to purchase.

The other key issue to bear in mind regarding life insurance is that you must qualify for the policy based upon your health and age. Once you have qualified for a life insurance policy and are past the contestable period, which is usually two years, then even if your health subsequently deteriorates your rating classification remains the same.

Generally, buy term insurance where your need is substantial and your budget is small. Buy cash value insurance where the need is permanent, whether death occurs tomorrow or 50 years from tomorrow.

With term policies, look for the option to convert to a cash value policy. You may never need this feature, but it is worthwhile to have this option. Generally, policies will let you convert on a guaranteed basis, that is at the same risk class and without a new physical, until either age 65 (ideal) or with some term policies only for the length of the term, i.e. 10 years, 20 years, etc.

A feature that is very valuable to have on a life policy is what is known as a "living benefit rider". This rider is offered by many carriers and depending upon the language, will pay out a part of the death benefit to the insured while living if the insured has a terminal illness. Admittedly, this is not a scenario that anyone wants to occur, but if the circumstances warrant, it can be very useful. The benefit is that the insured can pay bills, pay for care, and even take a "last hurrah" trip if able, without having to borrow or use other assets. A further benefit is that the living benefit rider is not a viatical settlement, meaning that the insured's family will still get the balance of the policy proceeds, less an interest factor.

The existence of the living benefit rider may be a compelling reason for a person to keep a life insurance policy in force even if he or she has little or no further requirement for the death benefit for heirs or to pay off debt. The living benefit rider can provide a pool of capital during a time of terminal illness and does help the insured avoid having to sell another asset at a fire sale price if the illness happens to coincide with a downturn in the markets.

The carriers developed these riders in response to the rise in the viatical settlement companies that sprang up in the 1980's. Since life insurance only requires an insurable interest at the time of the inception of the policy and not at time of claim, the insurance company cannot stop a person from selling his or her policy once it is issued and in force. Needless to say, the carriers do not like an uninterested party owning a policy on the life of their insured.

The key disadvantage with a viatical settlement is that the insured gets a fraction of the face value now and the viatical company and its investors get the balance of the policy when the insured dies. My own opinion is that there is more hype than reality to viatical settlements and they, like reverse mortgages, should be carefully scrutinized before utilized. In any event, the living benefit rider offered by most reputable life companies may well preclude the need for a viatical settlement.

Disability Insurance

Disability income insurance is designed to replace a part of your income should you become disabled. Generally the insurance carriers will not issue you a benefit greater than 60% or 66% of your income as the carriers do not want to provide an incentive for someone to falsely claim a disability and in essence retire at or near their full income. The disability policies are designed to prevent a financial catastrophe while you recover and rehabilitate.

Some large employers will offer a disability plan and many states have a short-term disability plan. Individual policies will generally be issued to coordinate with any company and/or government benefits. Although Social Security disability may be available for workers covered under Social Security, be aware that Social Security only approves about one third of the claims it receives. Generally, in order to qualify for Social Security disability, the disability must be permanent and/or expected to result in your death.

Therefore, Social Security disability will generally not be available for the person who, for example, breaks a leg and is off work for six months but is expected to make a full recovery.

Disability income policies generally are the most difficult of any form of insurance for which to qualify. This is due to the fact that a person might have a medical condition such as a bad back that is not necessarily life-threatening immediately but which could have a significant impact on their ability to work. Also your occupation will significantly impact both price and availability of an individual disability policy. Generally speaking white collar workers with desk jobs who have less work related exposure to risk will be offered a policy at more favorable terms than a blue-collar worker who faces some physical hazards. Some occupation classes simply are not offered disability insurance at all, such as crop dusters.

If you can qualify for and afford the premiums, an individual disability policy can make sense. Look for the phrases non-cancelable and guaranteed renewable. These two phrases mean that the policy premiums cannot go up (unless you have bought what is known as a graded premium policy) and that your policy cannot be canceled due to changes in your health.

Long-Term Care Insurance

Long-Term care insurance is a relative newcomer to the insurance world. The policies were designed to address the issue of an aging population. In many cases we simply become more frail as we grow older and require what is known as custodial care. Custodial care covers activities of daily living such as eating, bathing, dressing and mobility. Many people are under the impression that Medicare will pay for long-term care or nursing care facilities. Medicare only pays for what is known as skilled nursing facilities.

Thank God I Paid Cash For The Rolls!

These are generally the types of care facilities one might go to following a major illness or operation. They are not what we would more commonly refer to as a nursing home where someone is getting custodial care simply because either due to frailty or a medical condition, they can no longer live at home. Additionally, Medicare generally does not pay for home health care.

In selecting a long-term care policy, generally speaking, look for a policy that will pay a benefit both in an accredited nursing home or care facility and one that will also pay for home health care. We often think that people go to nursing homes following a major illness after surgery, but often it is the case that an elderly person has simply become too frail to live at home or can no longer feed, clothe and bathe alone and requires assistance.

A policy that provides a home health care benefit may make it financially feasible for the person to stay in their home for a longer period of time. Most people prefer to live at home as long as possible.

A key benefit of having a long-term care policy is that even if the policy doesn't cover the entire cost of the daily or monthly nursing home charges, the very existence of the policy means that you are a private pay patient rather than a public assistance patient. This will generally give you access to a wider range of care facilities as some care facilities do not except Medicare or Medicaid only patients. Of course this does not guarantee that as a private pay patient you will necessarily end up with a better care facility or better care, but it does give you more of an advantage at the outset.

An additional benefit of simply having a policy may be that your carrier will have a case manager who can help you locate care providers. This benefit will vary from company to company; ask your agent what, if any, case coordination is offered. This may not be a

160

panacea, but it provides the potential of having someone to help evaluate and secure care providers.

The issue of how much of a policy to buy, as with most insurance planning, is a trade-off between how much premium is reasonable and how much of the cost one can afford to self-insure.

In a perfect world where the premium is not an issue, you would buy a lifetime benefit policy, with a compound inflation rider, with a fairly large per day dollar benefit; say $200-$250. However, the premium for such comprehensive coverage may be rather substantial.

The next best strategy is to purchase a policy that provides at least a three-year benefit. Since 80% of nursing home stays average 2 ½ years, a three-year benefit policy, statistically speaking, will provide a long enough duration with the exception of a prolonged case of dementia. Although not perfect, this compromise provides at least some benefit and the reasonable duration.

Another way to reduce your premium is to select a longer waiting period before benefits begin. The difference between a 30 day waiting period and a 90 or 100 day waiting period for the same dollar benefit and duration can be substantial. The idea here is that you have self insured the first three months of care. (This is why you have a savings account for emergencies!)

The primary goal of a long-term care policy is that you don't want to have to deplete all of your assets in the final years of life. Even a long-term care policy that does not cover all of the cost of care will at least slow down the rate of depletion of assets.

Medical Insurance

The whole issue of health insurance is one of continuous debate in the United States and may very well change over the

ensuing decades, based upon political and economic circumstances.

The current options are either to work for an employer who
furnishes medical insurance or to purchase an individual policy.
Most employers now require their employees to pay part of the
cost of the premiums. Generally, the employee can cover his or
her dependents, usually for an extra premium. Some employers
will offer a cafeteria or Section 125 plan that may make the premium cost income tax deductible to the employee. This helps to
offset part of the premium expense.

Most group medical insurance is offered on a guaranteed issue
basis as long as you enroll upon meeting the eligibility requirements, such as a 90 day waiting period after your hire date, or at
the annual open enrollment period. Always learn and understand
the rules for applying for coverage for yourself and your dependents. Never cancel existing coverage until you have verified that
the new coverage is in effect. Ask for help from your company's
human resource department or the insurance carrier.

If you leave an employer for any reason, be sure to determine if
you are eligible for COBRA, which is a program that lets you continue your employer's coverage for 18 to 30 months depending
upon circumstances. You pay the entire premium so the premium
will be higher than what you had paid whilst an employee. The
benefit of COBRA is that you do not have to qualify. The downside, of course, is the higher premium cost.

The issue for individual purchase is much tougher. Generally
speaking, you must qualify for individual coverage. A carrier does
not have to accept you if you have a pre-existing condition and they
do not want to "buy a claim". Even a fairly minor medical com-
plaint can be a red flag if it can lead to a more serious condition.

Essentially, the carriers are evaluating the likelihood of a claim and how much their liability will total. The health care reform act will change this after 2014, assuming that its provisions remain in place and are not repealed either legislatively or judicially. If the current legislation remains in place, after 2014, you will be able to buy individual coverage regardless of preexisting conditions.

If you can qualify for an individual plan and you save consistently, consider using a Health Savings Plan. An HSA plan will have a very high deductible and therefore a lower premium. With an HSA, you can then open an HSA savings account at a bank or credit union. The money you put in the account is tax deductible. You use the money to meet medical expenses until you reach the deductible of the insurance plan. The beauty of the HSA is that any money not used in a particular year stays in the account and is available for future years. The HSA is useful for the healthy individual who has low utilization of medical services and has the discipline to save the annual amount into the savings account.

There are some state sponsored guaranteed issue programs. The two big issues with most are that you may have to wait until there is space in the plan and, more importantly, the premiums will be substantially more than regular individual policies.

As you reach age 65 and if you are eligible for Medicare, be sure to enroll in Parts A, B and D in a timely manner. Generally, you can purchase a Medicare supplement policy on a guaranteed issue basis if you apply within six months of enrolling in Medicare Part B. This is especially important if you have a pre-existing condition. Medicare supplement policies are now standardized, using a letter system, so you can compare premiums on "an apples for apples" basis.

With both enrollment in Medicare and the purchase of any supplemental policy, pay careful attention to the timing of when you must apply. As a rule of thumb, do your research by age 64 ½, so that you have a clear understanding of the sequence of enrolling and you have time to shop for and evaluate any supplemental coverage without an impending deadline.

As a general rule, I recommend having a Medicare supplement and the Part D supplement policy. Medicare has both a deductible and co-payments and typically does not cover all of actual charges. The supplement can help pay some (or all) of the deductible and co-payments. The better Medicare supplement plans will also pay some or all of the difference between "Medicare approved charges" and the actual amount charged by your hospital or care provider.

For seniors, get help and advice from a trusted agent or broker. Always get references from any representative who is unknown to you before doing business. Never do business with anyone if you feel pressured. If you do not have a relationship with an agent or broker, ask for referrals from several people who are qualified to make such a recommendation.

Due to the issues of cost and availability, at some point the current system may change from what we know today. The biggest stumbling block is cost. Americans want and use more health care than what the total contribution from individuals, companies, and the federal and state governments can afford. That said, the sea change that is occurring is that corporations are starting to want to get out of providing medical insurance in order to give US companies a more level playing field with companies domiciled in countries that have some sort of national health care system. As that pressure builds, perhaps a uniform system will emerge. It may be that a two-tiered system will emerge with a basic health care insurance provided for everyone and then the option of buying a supplemental policy that may provide greater coverage or faster access to care and cover more advanced heroic medical procedures. *Stay tuned.*

Property Casualty Insurance

Automobile insurance is often mandated by the various states as a condition of registering the car. You are usually required to carry liability (in case you injury someone or property). Comprehensive and collision are designed to cover the car. Carry high liability limits in order to protect your assets in the event you are at fault. Some states have "no-fault" systems.

Homeowners insurance is generally required by a lender for any home with a mortgage and certainly a good idea for those fortunate enough to have paid off their mortgage. Renter's insurance is advisable if you are renting and have valuable personal property.

In the case of both auto and homeowners, purchase higher liability limits (to help protect your assets if you are liable). You may be able to control costs by using a higher deductible. This is a good option if you are a good saver and have the "rainy day fund" to meet a high deductible. The benefit is that you have lower on-going premiums. Use the premium savings to establish and replenish your rainy day fund. A good casualty agent or broker can give you the options and help you determine the "sweet spot" that is the right balance between premiums and deductibles.

The key evaluation is to insure the catastrophic risk. It is more important to have your home insured for replacement cost than have a lower deductible. It is easier to absorb the deductible than pay for a new house!

Liability (personal and professional)

For those with a reasonable amount of net worth, ask your casualty agent about purchasing a liability umbrella. The appropriate amount will be determined by your net worth. This can be added to your auto or homeowners policy, generally at a fairly low premium. The concept here is that you are better protected against a catastrophic loss.

Certain professions have their respective malpractice or errors and omissions insurance. In many cases the appropriate coverage is mandatory to practice the profession. Check with your industry trade association or colleagues in your industry or a qualified insurance broker who specializes in your industry.

On Your Own – Or With an Advisor?

With the advent of the internet and on-line brokerage, many people today may find that they do not need or want to pay for advice from a financial planner or advisor. The decision of whether to use an advisor or not will generally depend upon your temperament, knowledge, inclination and time to pay attention to your finances. There is no right or wrong answer here: the point is to make a conscious decision whether or not to hire professionals. In today's world it is not uncommon for people to perform some financial activities on their own and use advisors for tasks and aspects for which they do not have the knowledge or time to complete.

If you do choose to engage a financial planner or a certified public accountant, or insurance agent or broker, always check the person's background. Secure a referral from a trusted source or ask the prospective advisor for a list of references. In addition to professional competence, look for someone with whom you are compatible and with whom you can build a good working relationship.

If you manage your finances on your own, keep up to date, get research from a variety of competent sources and monitor your accounts.

CHAPTER 8

LEGACY

Estate Planning

If you have done things right, at some point, you will have an estate to manage and to pass on to your heirs, or leave for a legacy.

Estate planning offers an opportunity to ensure that your wealth serves the people and charitable causes that are important to you. Depending upon the size of your estate and the estate tax laws in effect at the time of your passing, there may be a federal and possibly a state estate tax to pay. Since tax laws and tax rates change periodically, it is vital for you to consult with your accountant and estate tax attorney, especially any time there is a major change in the tax code. Beside the "hard facts" of an estate plan, such as the composition of one's assets and their value, there are also the "soft facts" of the estate planning process. The "soft facts" can include such issues as inter family relationships and one's emotions surrounding money and death. Here is an example of hard and soft facts to illustrate the point.

Under current law, if you leave all of your estate to a qualified charity, your estate will not pay any estate tax. However, if you do so, with no other planning, your heirs receive nothing. In this case, you beat the tax man, but your heirs get shortchanged as well. So the right plan may not always be the most tax efficient, but rather will be a balance of often competing goals.

Besides the pure "number crunching", there are emotional and balance factors. For example, if you have a family-owned business or farm and have some children who will continue the business, but others who will not, you have to decide how to be fair. If the bulk of your estate is the business and you leave it to son number 1, then what about son number 2, and your daughter? In such cases, you may want to leave other assets to heirs who will not be part of the business. If the other assets are insufficient to result in an equal share, then consider using a life insurance policy to help equalize the estate.

> *The key with estate planning is to start with the goal in mind and then to the extent practical, work to achieve that result.*

"Yours, Mine and Ours" - Planning for the Blended Family

A further issue is what is known as the "blended family" where a couple has children from a prior marriage. Readers of a certain age may remember the movie "Yours, Mine and Ours" starring Lucille Ball and Henry Fonda. In the movie, both characters had a number of children from their first marriage and then by the end of the movie have a baby of their own. This is a very common occurrence in modern life and needs to be intentionally evaluated and proper planning done to ensure that the desired result occurs.

My great-uncle Olin had been married for over 55 years when his first wife Elizabeth died. Olin and Elizabeth had four children. He re-married at the age of 81. By making proper arrangements, Uncle Olin was able to provide for his second wife had she survived him, while still providing for his own children. This was accomplished by a trust which could provide income for his second spouse and leave the remainder of his estate to his children. (As it turned out, Uncle Olin lived to age 101 and outlived his second wife.) The key is that a plan was in place that would have accomplished the desired result.

Consider for a moment what might happen for a couple in their second marriage without any planning in place. If one spouse dies without a will, then all of his or her assets will go to the surviving spouse. When that second spouse dies, his or her assets will go to that spouse's children and not to the first spouse's children, even though some of the assets were originally the other spouse's property and would have otherwise gone to that spouse's biological children had he or she not re-married.

The solution is to have a will or trust that might provide income and or use of the couple's residence for the surviving spouse during his or her lifetime and then upon the second spouse's death, have the assets go to the children of that spouse. This is especially useful where a couple has married during their "golden years" and wishes to provide for both the surviving spouse and ensure that their respective children get their own parent's property.

Good estate planning can help you determine how to treat children and step-children and provide for a surviving spouse. Get help and advice from a qualified estate planning attorney to both determine the appropriate legal structure and to prepare the appropriate documents. Review your legal documents periodically and in particular anytime there is a life event such as the birth of a child or grandchild, or death or divorce.

"Planning for Non-Traditional Couples"

A non-traditional couple may be a man and a woman who live together as a couple but are not legally married or it may be a same gender couple. In some cases, the couple may have entered into a civil union or domestic partnership or similar arrangement as offered by that couple's state of residence. As of this writing, the status of same gender couples varies widely from state to state, from legal strangers, to civil unions or domestic partnerships, to marriage at the state level. A Supreme Court ruling in 2013 appears to grant recognition at the federal level, although legal challenges continue. Due to this legal disparity, it is vital for such couples to have a plan in place and have a competent attorney who is familiar with the laws in that couple's state of residence prepare the appropriate wills and/or trust and consider a durable power of attorney and directive to physician. Otherwise, at a critical moment, such as a life threatening illness or death, the couple may find themselves as legal strangers and be precluded from making medical or financial decisions for each other. The issue of same gender relations has been and will continue to be hotly debated and it is likely that the legal landscape on this issue may change over the ensuing decades. Any future legal changes, whether more restrictive or more favorable for such couples, should then be evaluated and any plans or documents be revised accordingly.

Any couple that has a civil union or domestic partnership that moves to another state must determine whether the current state will recognize the former state's arrangements and make new legal arrangements accordingly. Again, consult with an attorney who is qualified to advise on such matters.

"Table for One?"

Single people need estate planning! In the good old days, there used to be a profession known as a "matchmaker". Sadly this profession is now about as rare as a unicorn and many people find themselves permanently single. Furthermore, some people who are presently married may find themselves single later in life due to either death of their spouse or divorce. So whether widowed, divorced or never married, the single person must plan. A durable power of attorney is important as it states who has the authority to look after your finances if you are too ill to attend to them. A "Directive to Physician" (sometimes referred to as a 'Living Will') will state your wishes as to whether you do or do not want heroic medical care in the event of a serious illness or accident.

Just as important as it is to have the legal documents in place, single people should also develop a network of professionals and friends who can assist with various tasks, especially as we get older. On a cruise through the Panama Canal, I had dinner with four women from Indiana, all widows who were traveling together. At home, they would call each other at 9:00 am each morning to ensure they were all right. If anyone failed to answer her phone, the others would summon help immediately. This sort of informal network is a godsend in an emergency and such friendships have a tremendous emotional value. Single people should cultivate such friendships.

"Pretending It's Not There Won't Make it Go Away"

There is an old saying in Italian that translated is "Everyone wants to go to Heaven, but nobody wants to die". Regardless of your domestic situation, you must plan for the event which we all hope is much later rather than sooner. I have worked with clients over the years who would not buy life insurance or have an attorney prepare a will because they thought that talking about death would hasten their own! The subject of death can bring about emotional issues or religious concerns and is never an easy subject to discuss. However, everyone is better off making decisions and arrangements long before the event is at hand. Good planning and the appropriate legal framework can help you and your heirs avoid needless expense and help to take the financial strain out of a very emotional time.

Charitable Giving and Legacy Planning

People with larger estates may find at some point in their life time that they would like to provide for a cause that is near and dear to their hearts. Charitable giving can be done both during lifetime and at death. If done during lifetime the donor may be able to structure a plan that provides income and will enjoy the satisfaction of seeing the charity benefit from his or her largess during lifetime. For those who require the use of all of their capital and income during their lifetimes a charitable bequest at death may be a more suitable disposition.

Even a donor of relatively modest means can provide a bequest to a charity. Here are some examples of planning techniques that may be used.

Charitable Remainder Trusts

Life insurance may be used in one of three ways for a charitable bequest. The most straightforward is to name a charity as a beneficiary for all or part of a life insurance policy. Under this scenario the donor retains ownership of the policy. Although the premiums are not deductible because the donor owns the policy, it gives the donor the flexibility to change the beneficiary if need be during his or her lifetime and to access cash values if available during lifetime.

A second method is for the charity to apply for and own the life insurance policy. The donor then makes a contribution to the charity which in turn pays a premium. Gets structured properly the contribution to the charity will be deductible. (A word of caution here: There was a period of time when some organizations would sell life insurance policies owned by the charity where most of the death benefit would be payable to the donor's heirs. This was essentially a scam to provide tax-deductible life insurance to a non-charitable beneficiary. The IRS has disallowed such transactions. Life insurance premiums are only deductible where the charity both owns the policy and is the sole beneficiary.

A third methodology for using life insurance to assist with charitable planning is to use it as a wealth replacement. In this case the donor has made a lifetime request to a charity of some property or asset and is receiving an income stream. The donor has given the asset irrevocably to the charity; none of those dollars are available to his or her beneficiaries. The donor may use some of the income stream to pay the premiums on a life insurance policy. The life insurance policy proceeds then replace some or all of the value of the donated property to the donor's heirs. This technique is a win-win-win. The charity gets the donated property. The donor gets the income during his or her lifetime and some income tax savings. The donor's heirs get the insurance proceeds in cash.

This technique is often used where the donor has a highly appreciated piece of property or assets and gives it to a charity. This avoids capital gain tax if properly structured. The life insurance policy will be set up in an irrevocable life insurance trust which is not part of the donor estate and the death benefit will be both income tax-free and estate tax-free to the beneficiaries. Under this scenario the donor has saved capital gains tax during his or her lifetime, has provided a legacy to the charity and has provided income and estate tax-free money to the beneficiaries. As always, consult with a qualified accountant and an attorney who are familiar with charitable trusts.

Charitable Foundation

In addition to bequests to a specific charity a very wealthy donor may choose to establish a charitable foundation. This gives both the donor during his or her lifetime and the managers of the foundation after the donor's lifetime the option and flexibility to change the recipients of the charitable donations. For example, the donor may have an interest in education. By setting up a private foundation the foundation might give a scholarship to individual students one year and provided grants to a college or university another year. Or, the donor might want to benefit a number of charities or might have a specific social or religious viewpoint and want the flexibility to be able to change the charitable contributions if the charity changes its emphasis or viewpoint in the ensuing decades.

By having funds in a private foundation, rather than giving the corpus directly and irrevocably to a specific charity, either the donor during lifetime or his or her successor trustees can change the charitable recipients to support those organizations who met the donor's objectives.

Generally speaking, charitable foundations are set up only by very wealthy donors where there is both sufficient revenue to pay for professional management and still have an adequate annual income to use to achieve the charitable objectives. Charitable foundations must meet minimum distribution requirements each year as set forth by the IRS. They cannot be a sham transaction to avoid paying income tax; they must be legitimate.

EPILOGUE

The Neo-Feudalist

I am often amazed by the two schools of thought one will hear during tumultuous times. One commentator will spin out a tale of doom and gloom and project how all of the trends indicate that very soon we will all go back to growing vegetables and raising chickens in the backyard because the entire financial system will have totally collapsed. The next commentator (often from my own industry) will give a very ivory tower or "smell of the lamp" speech or write a commentary on how everything is going to be "peachy keen" and rosy. I often wonder how to reconcile these two divergent views.

It is irresponsible for me as a financial planner to go off on a tangent and tell a client or my reader or an audience that it's all doom and gloom and you should put your money under a mattress and prepare for Armageddon. Conversely, it is also irresponsible for me to simply trot out the platitude "Well, these things go in cycles and it will all come back so don't worry." Both of these approaches are frankly far too simplistic.

A further debate that rages in the United States is the one between a wide open laissez-faire "Cowboy Capitalism" and "Nanny State Socialism". The two schools of thought are presented as an "either/or" choice of absolutes. The reality, of course, is that this is a false choice between two ideals. The United States is a capitalist society that uses regulation to temper the inevitable boom and bust cycle of capitalism and attempts to pull the reins in on human greed.

In a pure laissez-faire system there would be no regulation of the markets, no protections for consumers from unscrupulous business practices, no protection for businesses from unscrupulous practices of their competitors or business partners either. So a purely wide open system can't work. In the same way, our society could not function if we did not have laws against robbery or murder and had no mechanism to protect against and punish those crimes. Otherwise, we would have anarchy.

For instance if there had not been FDIC insurance in place during the crash of 2008 it is a safe bet to say that by September 30, 2008 there would not have been so much as a plug nickel sitting in any bank anywhere in the United States. The existence of federal insurance gave depositors enough assurance so that they continued to leave their funds in the banks. The opposite was true in the US stock market where investors voted with their feet and trillions of dollars sprouted legs and walked (ran?) out of the stock market and on to the sidelines.

Conversely, it is unlikely in the United States that we would ever evolve to a model where the state owned all of the means of production in a socialistic model. The state owned model failed spectacularly in many countries throughout the world during the 20th century and even those countries today that use the state owned model are evolving to at least a partially privatized system. We have seen how an aggressive state owned model discourages individual initiative and stifles creativity and economic growth. So a pure socialist model does not work.

The debate is really about how much and to what extent the capital markets can and should be regulated. Just as food safety, clean air and water and other standards have been set and are enforced, the same must be true for the financial system. Anything that looks and smells and acts like a financing mechanism needs to be treated as such. There must reasonable underwriting standards and transparency and the issuer should have adequate capital reserves in the same manner that banks set aside a capital reserve when they book a new loan.

Proper regulation does not mean the end of competition, but rather reasonable regulation hopefully keeps unscrupulous people and companies at bay and gives businesses and consumers the confidence to participate in the capital market system. Of course the existence of regulations does not prevent bad actors from attempting to circumvent the rules. Nor does the existence of auditing and accounting standards, compliance reviews, and regulation prevent all problems from occurring. However, having these rules and enforcement systems in place is the only way to create confidence in the system.

As individuals we must always establish ourselves to in the strongest possible financial position with both a protection on the down side of the economic wheel and a position to benefit from growth. One might view this somewhat pessimistically as "neo-feudalism", but in essence each person does have to incorporate some aspects of feudalism.

In the Middle Ages, the lord of a castle was the master of his own little world. He was responsible to himself, his family and his vassals. When trouble threatened, the drawbridges would be raised to keep the "infidels" out.

We all have to think, at least in part, in that same manner. By that I mean that ultimately, each person is responsible for his or her own financial security.

The reality then is that at any given time there will be some trends that are very favorable and others that are very negative. There will be periods of time when most of the trends are positive and other periods when most are negative. In many cases, the business cycle will mean that things do come back but it does not always mean that everything comes back or that everything comes back in the same manner and format that it did previously.

This is not to take a wishy-washy middle ground approach but rather to emphasize the need to continually monitor and rethink or adjust your plan based on circumstances and more importantly to the extent that any of us can, to try and anticipate where trends are going, what industries or markets are headed towards expansion and what areas are perhaps headed toward decline and to make appropriate changes.

Hope – "An Anthem for Our Times"

The word hope has perhaps been overused, but I'm going to conclude this treatise on surviving and thriving through an economic crisis with this very word, hope.

In the midst of all this economic meltdown, one fine spring evening, I performed the very happy annual task of serving as the Master of Ceremonies for the Porterville Panther Band. One of the selections that night was a piece written by a 17-year-old trumpeter in the band, Kory McMaster entitled "An Anthem for Our Times." He dedicated the piece to teachers and doctors and nurses and all the people who work so hard to make our society work. And as I reflected upon the spirit of the title and the dedication and compared it with the anxiety and despair that many of us adults had felt in these moments of crisis during the economic meltdown, I thought how uplifting and encouraging it was for a 17-year-old student with his whole life ahead of him to compose an original piece of music and arrange it for a concert band to play and to acknowledge what is good about life and offer hope for the future and how all of us could take a lesson from this example of perseverance.

One the other end of the spectrum, a month later, I attended the annual Rolls-Royce Owners Club picnic, held at a member's home in Vineyard Valley in the wine country of California. He proudly displayed the progress made on his small railroad, another 1/3 of a mile of track laid down by a man in his 80's and using a cane cleverly fashioned from PCV pipe to help him walk with his arthritis. Yet his voice was clear and strong and the smile on his face beamed as he talked about his railroad and the gizmo installed in the mill that churned the most delicious homemade ice cream.

At the conclusion of the picnic on that warm June day, I pointed my Rolls-Royce southbound on Highway 29 and looked through the windscreen, over the bonnet to the mascot - the Spirit of Ecstasy - also known as The Flying Lady, alighted gracefully atop the grill of the motorcar. And I reflected on the lives and legacy of the people who created the Rolls-Royce motorcar.

I thought about Eleanor Thornton, the woman who was the model for the iconic mascot, the Spirit of Ecstasy. She died tragically when the SS Persia was torpedoed off the coast of Crete in December, 1915 during World War I. And what of The Honorable Charles S. Rolls, one of the founders, who died in the first fatal airplane crash in Great Britain in 1910 at the age of only 32? And what of Henry Royce, OBE, the perfectionist, hard-working engineer who designed the early Rolls-Royce motorcars who had a near fatal illness in 1911, yet carried on for another 20 years as a semi-invalid, during which time he designed the Merlin engine which would play a major role in the aircraft used by the British in saving that nation during World War II?

Eleanor Thornton's and Charles Rolls' all too brief lives remind us of how precious life is and that we must savor each day. The life and example of Henry Royce counsels us all to give our best effort at whatever we set our hand to and to persevere, even when times are tough.

SO WHETHER ONE IS 18 OR 80, THERE IS ALWAYS HOPE.

The other area, without sounding too "Pollyanna-ish", is that as long as each of us has breath we must persevere. There is a line in one of the chapters of "The Greatest Salesman on Earth" by Og Mandino that emphasizes the need for persistence, *"I will avoid despair but if this disease of the mind should infect me then I will work on in despair. I will ignore the obstacles at my feet and keep mine eyes on the goals above my head, for I know that where dry desert ends, green grass grows"*

So the key is no matter who you are or what your circumstances are there must be at least one thing, however small it may seem, there must be at least one thing that you can do today, this minute, this week, this month that can begin to make a change in your economic life and by extension improve your overall well-being.

As Woody Woodson so eloquently put it may years ago, may I echo his words and wish for you, dear reader, "Happiness and emotional stability beyond compare".

Be Part of the Sequel!

Do you have your own story of financial struggle, survival or success? You are invited to be a part of the next book! Whether you made a fortune, had a "Failure to Proceed", or anything in between, we want to hear about it. If there is an area in the book that you would like to know more about, please send me your stories and ideas. All stories will be kept confidential and if we use your story or idea, we will ask permission before publication and will change names and details to ensure your privacy.

Please e-mail your stories to Eric S. Ball, at eric.ball@kmsfinancial.com. You may also telephone our office at (559) 784-0957. Website www.eballwealth.com.

GLOSSARY OF FRACTURED FINANCIAL TERMS

Baby Dollars – Term used to describe interest earned. When that interest is left to compound and the interest earns interest, then we speak of "baby dollars having baby dollars". Small amounts of money left to compound or re-invested can grow to large amounts over time.

Clean Money – Term used to describe funds used to pay the taxes due on a Roth IRA conversion. Clean money means using outside dollars that are not part of the IRA.

Dead Money – Refers to money that is earning or has earned no return. For example, most money in the stock market in the first decade of the 21st century was dead money in that there was no return made and in many cases the principal amount diminished.

Dead Money Decade – The period of time from 2000 to 2010. The value of stocks, bonds and real estate plummeted, taking earnings with it, so that most investors had less at the end of the decade than at the beginning. All assets earned made no money and thus the label "dead money". Thus, the decade is to forever to be known as the "Dead Money Decade". RIP!

Dirty Money – Refers to money used to pay the taxes on a Roth IRA conversion using the IRA's own money. This approach defeats the purpose of doing the Roth IRA as there will be tax due on the "dirty money" (and the 10% penalty if under age 59 ½) and those dollars are lost and will not be available to earn a return in the account. Never use dirty money to effect a Roth conversion.

Failure To Proceed – While technically an automotive phrase, it can be used to describe any situation where something doesn't work. It makes a nice little shorthand and always elicits sympathy and a knowing nod from those in the know. Knowing and preparing for a potential FTP can help to reduce the frequency and severity of same.

Grunt Work – These are all the unpleasant tasks of life that must be done, some necessary, some imposed on us by others. It may be actual physical work as the name implies, but may also be an emotionally difficult task. The key with grunt work is that often some big goal requires grunt work for its accomplishment.

Marginal Tax Rate – Refers to the rate of federal income tax that one pays on the next dollar of earned income. For example, in 2012, a single taxpayer with a taxable income of $35,350 would be in the 15% income tax bracket. Any taxable income above that amount would then be taxed at the next bracket of 25%. If the taxpayer earned $35,351 they would be in a 25% marginal tax bracket, even though only the one dollar above $35,350 would be taxed at 25%.

Money Heaven – This is the place where dollars go during market crashes. This bit of gallows humor can sometimes help ease the pain of market losses.

Needless Enrichment – This phrase is used to describe any financial transaction wherein the party receiving the money gets far more money than what the item or service is worth or deserved, especially the deserved aspect. Put simply, it is where the price tag is huge and the value received by the person who pays the money is little or nothing and unearned and undeserved by the recipient.

For example, a CEO of a large corporation that has lost a ton of money during the year that still gets a seven or eight figure bonus has received needless enrichment. Points paid to 'buy down" the interest rate on a mortgage are always needless enrichment. Any time you pay a "convenience fee" to buy a ticket to some event (no "fee" is ever "convenient"), or any single person who has to pay a "single supplement" for a tour or cruise has given the recipient of that fee "needless enrichment". And the most egregious example of needless enrichment is any overtime parking ticket that has ever been issued anywhere on earth. Cars are sacred. Period.

Good financial planning entails recognizing and then reducing and eliminating any and all incidents of needless enrichment.

Psychic Income – This term was coined by an erstwhile compliance officer who used the term to describe anything that happens to a person from a non-financial perspective that makes them feel good. For example, applause given to an actor for a bravura performance is known as psychic income. A compliment given to you for some achievement, especially from someone you love or admire, is psychic income. It is income that cannot be deposited into a bank but rather income that is deposited into one's own brain and heart.

Programmed Seepage – This term is also technically a British automotive one, (British cars never leak oil, but they do have "programmed seepage") but when applied to financial planning it refers to minor expenses that are inevitable in daily living. It is the "miscellaneous" category on your budget. Sometimes it is frivolous or impulse purchases at a checkout line. It is a relative of needless enrichment, but not as egregious. It is the $20 your neighbor borrowed but never paid back. It is money that seems to sprout legs and walk away. A certain amount of programmed seepage is inevitable. The key is to recognize it and minimize it where practical.

Sleep Factor – This term refers to the emotional level of comfort that an investor has with a particular investment or asset. If you wake up in the middle of the night and can't get back to sleep because you are worried about the value of a particular investment or if you make a change in an investment because you cannot handle the volatility that means the investment does not meet your own personal sleep factor. The level of intensity of the sleep factor will always be different for each individual. The key is to always be aware of one's own personal sleep factor in making investment decisions.

Stupid Money – This occurs where a person has so much money that they can do "inadvisable", i.e. stupid things with their money, yet they still have so much money that the loss has no impact on their financial lives. For example, spending a small fortune to restore an unsteady car where the value gained does not equal the expense. After the meltdown of '08, there is probably a lot less stupid money.

Tax In-Efficient – This describes any strategy or financial transaction where the result is a tax cost that is higher than necessary. An example of tax inefficiency would be to contribute $1000 into an IRA account when the individual is in the 10% marginal tax bracket and then takes the funds out when the person is in a 30% marginal bracket. Ignoring the interest factor for our example the person would save $100 when the funds were contributed but pay

$300 when the funds were withdrawn. This $200 net cost would be considered tax inefficient.

Wallet Emptying – The term used where something is extremely expensive. It may refer to something that is very expensive, but worth the cost, for example a college education at an expensive private university where the student goes on to enjoy a 40 year career doing something he or she really enjoys and makes a contribution to society.

Conversely, it may also be something that is very expensive and not worth the cost but sadly falls under the category of "needless enrichment". It may also be used to describe something that has to be done (fix the car, pay taxes) and can't be avoided. It is designed to invoke a light bit of mirth into an otherwise tough situation.

BIOGRAPHY

Eric S. Ball, CLU, ChFC, MSFS, CFP, is a third generation native Californian. Eric entered the financial services industry in 1981 with The Bankers Life. He established his own firm, Ball Wealth Management, in 2006 with offices in San Francisco and Porterville, California.

Eric earned his undergraduate degree in history from the University of California, Berkeley and his Masters in Financial Services from The American College, Bryn Mawr, Pennsylvania.

From the boardroom of corporate clients to the "Back Forty" with farmers and growers, to professionals, self-employed business owners, to retirees, Eric has worked with hundreds of individuals, business owners and corporate clients, specializing in financial planning and retirement plans.

The result of working with a diverse range of clients, from urban to rural, from generation X and Y, to Baby Boomers, to clients in their golden years, has given Eric a unique perspective on how people and their finances interact.

He is the past president of the Tulare-Kings Life Underwriters Association and currently serves on the board of the Tulare-Kings Estate Planning Council.

Thank God I Paid Cash For The Rolls!

Eric's civic activities include past president of the Rotary Club of Porterville, past president of the Porterville Chamber of Commerce and Master of Ceremonies for the Porterville Panther Band and other community events.

Eric is a frequent speaker on ocean liners and has spoken on six different cruise ship lines giving presentations on a wide variety of historical topics.

As a life long automotive enthusiast, Eric is the 2011-2012 Chairman of the Rolls-Royce Owners Club - Northern California Region. His other interests include singing, history and travel.